PRESIDENTIAL CAMPAIGNS

from Washington to Roosevelt

GEORGE MJRRAY MCCONNEL

Lire Books: New York

Presidential Campaigns: from Washington to Roosevelt
Copyright ©2017 Lire Books

Author: George Murray Mcconnel
Editor: Rachel Drice

Published Originally By Rand, Mcnally & Co; Chicago, New York, London
Copyright, 1908

Book Website: www.LireBooks.com
Email: info@LireBooks.com
Give feedback on the book at: feedback@LireBooks.com

ISBN-10: 1-939652-84-7
ISBN-13: 978-1-939652-84-3

A NOTE TO OUR READERS

We express our regret, if anyone takes offense to any language or imagery found within this publication. There are some words that may be considered politically incorrect or crude. For the literary and historical integrity of this publication, we have decided to leave each word as is.

Lire Books nor it's subsidiaries endorses any of the negative or derogatory attitudes. However these publications record the speech and manners of a particular region during a specific historical era. Transcription of this text has remained as close to a literal reproduction of the manuscript as possible. Punctuation, capitalization, paragraphing, and spelling of all words are retained as they appear in the original document.

Many people enjoy these publications as they are for pure reading enjoyment. Should you find any of the language personally offensives and decide text is not for you, it would be understandable if you chose not to continue reading.

HISTORICAL PERSPECTIVES

Taking historical perspective means understanding the social, cultural, intellectual, and emotional settings that shaped people's lives and actions in the past. At any one point, different historical actors may have acted on the basis of conflicting beliefs and ideologies, so understanding diverse perspectives is also a key to historical perspective-taking. Though it is sometimes called "historical empathy," historical perspective is very different from the common-sense notion of identification with another person. Indeed, taking historical perspective demands comprehension of the vast differences between us in the present and those in the past.

Historical Thinking Project
http://historicalthinking.ca/historical-perspectives

A PREFECTORY WORD

The knowledge acquired by the citizen of the United States of the drift and the spirit of the development of the institutions under which we live cannot be too broad. It may be so minutely accurate as to certain details as to lose touch with the spirit of the growth. It may be so meagre as to lead to readiness to accept any new device, born of a sudden exigency, and so become revolutionary by accident of ignorance.

The aim of this quasi historical review of our political development as regards electing our presidents, first printed in the New York Evening Telegram, is not so much mere dry, technical precision of statement as it is to put the reader in sympathetic touch with the spirit of that development. If there is another monograph with that aim it has escaped the attention of

The Author.

CONTENTS

CHAPTER I

First in War, in Peace, and in Men's Hearts

Late in the year 1788 the people of the United States had their first presidential election. It was the first "presidential campaign" in that quadrennial series in which there has been no interruption. That campaign was conducted within a narrow area, only one or two hundred miles wide, along the coast from Boston to Savannah, and enlisted the interest of a population of less than four millions. That of 1908 stretched over nearly double the latitude and ten times the longitude measured in miles, and stirred a population twenty times more numerous.

Vast as is this merely physical difference, that in the manner of conducting the campaign is relatively as wide, and in any "presidential year" it cannot be unprofitable to glance swiftly over the series of elections and observe the successive Step by which we have attained so wide a difference while nominally adhering quite closely to the original forms. The United States, under the "Articles of Confederation," had a nominal existence from A'farch 2, 1781, when those "Articles" went into effect, in a legal sense. In the sense of creating, or organizing, any actual national, or even political, entity they never "went into effect" at all. Each State of the league continued to do as it pleased even more capriciously than when they were held together by the pressure of foreign. war. In a broad sense the first presidential campaign may be said to have covered the more than seven years between the enactment and nominal. acceptance of the "Articles" and the first election under the Constitution, late in 1788. When that instrument was ratified by the necessary nine States, the necessity for something of the kind was practically admitted by all the people. It was felt that it was only fair that it should be put in operation by those who had formulated it, and that at its head should be placed the one man whose exalted character and whose sword had made possible this opportunity for the people to control their own governmental condition. The leadership of Washington had won political independence for the States and their people, and his leadership had been no less real and effective in determining the new governmental form. Others had said and written more, but no one or two or half a dozen of them all had exerted so real an influence in persuading the people to accept and try the result of their combined labors. Every one of the sixty-nine votes of the electors chosen at that first election was cast for him.

Fear of "one-man power," kingly in mode of action, though not in origin, and believed to tend, in strong hands, toward becoming hereditary, had been largely influential in leaving the old Confederation without any executive head. Fear of popular tumult and disorder and the consequent opening for a tyranny of the sword or of the blatant demagogue had as largely influenced the Constitution makers to devise the electoral system, whereby the people were sup-posed to select the wisest men, who, in turn, were empowered, as independently as the people chose them, to choose the President and Vice President. That is to say, they might vote, each of them, for two men, but no two of them necessarily for the same two men, and, among all they might vote for, that one having the largest number of votes, provided they made a majority of the electors, should be declared President, and that one having the next largest number of votes, whether a majority of the electors or not, should be Vice President.

No one of the Constitution makers, speaking from memory of the known record, seems to have seen that if only two electors should vote for the same man as second choice, and all the other electors should scatter their votes among as many as themselves, the man with two votes might be Vice President, though in a minority of only two in the whole body of electors. Au extreme case, but quite possible.

Nobody, either, has ever explained why the people are any better qualified to make choice of the "best men" to choose a President than to make choice of the one man sufficiently qualified to be President.

The overshadowing character and public service of -Washington precluded any such disaster in the first place, but the electoral vote for the second man should have been an instant warning of what might be possible. John Adams, who, it was scarcely open to doubt, stood second in public service to Washington only, received 34 votes, while 35 were scattered among ten other men, and so he became Vice President by a minority vote of the whole body.

Four years later Washington's character again gave him every electoral vote, increased now to 132 by increased population and an added number of states, and John Adams was again chosen Vice President, having received 77 votes. Oddly enough, the official record declares that he him-self as Vice President, in announcing the result declared himself elected Vice President "by a plurality of votes," although in fact he had received a clear majority of the whole college.

In this arrangement it was supposed that the people would not know for whom they were voting for executive officers, the electors being free to vote for whomsoever they might wish, since their believed high character and knowledge of men would enable them, presumably, to choose more intelligently than the body of the people could. As a matter of fact, every American voter knew that he was casting his vote in effect for 'Washington to be President, and so the sys-tem failed, in effect, on its first trial, though it happened, indeed, that in that case the people and their chosen electors were of one mind.

Thus far the spirit of party had entered very little into these elections, though it seems strange indeed that thoughtful men did not see that it must sooner or later inevitably do so. It had al-ready begun with the difference between those who advocated a strict construction of the constitution, led by Jefferson, the prevalence of whose then views would have assimilated the new government as closely as possible to the helpless old Confederation, and, on the other hand, the broad constructionists, led mainly by Hamilton, whose view was that the primary aim of the new government form was the erection of a nation worthy to stand among nations, and, therefore, that constitutional provisions should be construed so as to promote that paramount purpose wherever practicable to do so without plainly infringing on personal liberty or the rights of the states to manage, each for itself, its own domestic affairs.

This difference of construction of the organic law under which the United States has its being as a political entity has been the basis of every party which has exerted any real and lasting influence in our history, and will probably be the basis of every effective new one which may here-after come into being. This is true because it is primal in its character, resting on the constitution of human character as truly as the laws of material force, the centripetal and the centrifugal tendencies that keep life and order in the universe, rest on the constitution of matter. The due balance of these opposing forces maintains the planetary system. If either should overcome the other chaos would indeed be "come again." The heart of strict construction is the right and liberty of action of the individual man. That of broad construction is the superior right and liberty of action of the organized community of men, which it holds must be conceded and obeyed in order that individual liberty may be guaranteed to all alike, the weak as well as the strong. If either overcomes the other, human society, in any proper sense, is impossible.

In all human history whenever the community, the state, has grown to be greatly preponderant, some crushing form of despotism has been the result. When-ever the individual has come to be all, or practically all, and the organized community nothing, or near to nothing, some form of savagery has been the result. Upon a due balance of the two, as upon the balance of the opposing center-seeking and center-flying planetary forces in the universe depends the ordered universe, depends like-wise the existence of organized human society. In either case the undue preponderance of one must be followed by the appropriate and inevitable reaction.

Thus far the ordering of the new government had been wholly in the bands of those who sought the formation of a "strong government," or, as they soon came to be called, the Federalists.

CHAPTER II

The Third And Fourth Elections

During the eight years of Washington's Presidency the constructive Federalists, with the co-operation of many who were not of just that political bent—Jefferson himself was in Washing-ton's Cabinet—had succeeded in getting the government into practical action, and in a fashion, so far as organization then went, which has not only been continued until today substantially, but has furnished the model for those parts of government installed at 'a later day. The work of the makers of the constitution has won lavish encomiums from some of the world's most distinguished men, but the work of the men who shaped and put in motion the actual government which the constitution only described in outline, and who so did that work that it has needed no changes save expansion to meet a larger growth, was not a whit less wonderful in character or in the profound judgment and skill of its execution, yet history has not given to them the high credit to which they were entitled.

Though Washington was twice elected unanimously the lines of cleavage into parties showed themselves soon, and surprise has been expressed that they so soon developed acrimony and personal bitternesses far beyond those of recent years. There should be no surprise. Party itself, without the check of royal power or hereditary rank was new. Men were new to the free use of any political tools, and the tools they now found in their hands being new also, awkward use of tools was natural. Men entertained convictions often without knowing quite how to give the full reason for them. It is always easier to feel than to think, and it should not surprise us that making " the other side" appear wrong and wicked seemed to many the surest way of vindicating the righteousness of their own convictions. We are not yet free from this weakness.

The difference between strict and broad construction, or the seed of it, was present from the first, and, as has been before remarked, Jefferson rose at once into the leadership of the strict school, and upon the retirement of Washington at the end of his second term party lines on that basis became manifest at once. But cleavage had already shown itself within the Federal party. Its most noteworthy manifestation, perhaps, was iii the resistance of some in the party, under the leadership of Madison, to the proposed payment of the nation's debt to its soldiers in full, as it 110 been already, agreed to pay its debts to foreign creditors. The resistance was based on the assertion that to pay in full would entire to the benefit not so much of the soldiers as of speculators who had bought up the claims of the soldiers at heavy discount, and Madison's proposal was to pay in full only to original holders, and to pay to others only what they had paid. This was to make the nation take advantage of the misfortune of individuals, ignoring the real truth that the debt of the nation was the same, no matter who held the claims. It was substantially the same as the attempt, many years later, to pay the bonds of the nation after the Civil war in "greenbacks," because their holders had so paid for them. Madison's proposal did not prevail, but it helped along the dissension in the Federalist ranks, and by the time for the third Presidential election Jefferson's ambition and his genius for political organization had welded the strict constructionists into a compact and disciplined party, ready to make him President if it could.

And besides these natural and legitimate party differences there were personal animosities that exerted far more influence on public action than they should. Hamilton was an ideal captain of an aggressive party, but his imperious temperament demanded unquestioning obedience to himself as such. John Adams was not a man to yield obedience to anybody without the approval of his own independent judgment of the matter in which obedience was asked. He and Hamilton were antipathetic by nature. It was Hamilton's influence that had made Adams' vote so largely in a minority in the first election, and though Adams did not quite know all the truth he knew something of it. During Washington's first term the Senate was very equally divided between the Federal party and its yet unorganized opponents, and no

9

less than twenty times in this first Presidential term it fell to Adams' lot to give the casting vote on measures, most, if not all, of which had been originated and championed by Hamilton. Adams was as loyal a Federalist as Hamilton, and without that touch of commerce promoting as a reason for Federalism which sometimes seemed so large a part of Hamilton's reason. Every one of these twenty casting votes he gave for the Hamiltonian measures. Hamilton, though he knew that these votes were cast in obedience to Adams' own judgment and not at all as a. follower of him, Hamilton, as a leader, was yet so far placated by them that at the second election he ignored his antipathy to the man and Adams therefore had the fair electoral majority of his party.

But when the third election was at hand and Washington peremptorily refused to stand again, matters were different. Jefferson had consolidated his party of "stricts" and everybody knew that the Federalists had few votes among the people to spare. Hamilton knew that, though the party "leader of the leaders," he himself was not popular with the mass of his party, and he quietly acquiesced in the selection of Adams as one of the party candidates, universally understood as standing for the first place. Thomas Pinckney, of South Carolina, was chosen for the other, and by like understanding, the second place. But as yet electors voted for two men merely, the one having the largest number of votes to be President.

Hamilton at once set about talking and writing to Federalist electors, especially those from New England, that no Federal votes could be spared, that all must be cast for Adams and Pinckney, lest the so-called Democrats might win if any were thrown away, while if the two Federal candidates should have the same number of votes, by strict following of his advice, the choice between the two would merely fall to a Federalist House of Representatives.

On its face this was both fair and wise politics. Until after the electoral vote was announced Adams himself did not know how narrowly he escaped defeat. But it was quite well known to nearly all Federalist leading men, and probably as well known to Jefferson and his immediate followers, that some Southern Federalists would not vote for Adams, and accordingly South Carolina gave her eight votes for Jefferson and Pinckney, and Pennsylvania, then inclining southward far more than toward New England, gave two votes to Pinckney and but one to Adams. New England electors were more wary. They voted solidly for Adams, but for second place eighteen of them scattered their votes among three men, of whom Pinckney was not one. Had these eighteen electors, or even thirteen of them, taken the plausible and fair-seeming advice of Hamilton. Pinckney would have been President, and Adams would have been, for the third time, Vice President. Probably most clear seeing politicians of the time believed that this was the end for which Hamilton was working. Probably few suspected him of any willingness to elect Jefferson President, or even Vice President, yet his action gave Jefferson within three of as many votes as Adams, and actually made him Vice President.

During his term President Adams, as quite everybody now admits, served his country with distinguished ability. But he was soon made aware of the truth about Hamilton's action, and thenceforth, as long as Hamilton lived, the quarrel between them knew no lulls in acrid vehemence. Perhaps the

President's most invaluable service to his country was his making peace with the new French republic, early in 1800. That peace was, or ought to have been, as ardently desired by Hamilton as by any one, both as an American statesman and as a Federalist. But Mr. Adams did not consult him, Hamilton, about it, and brought it about in a way that demonstrated his independence of the party leader, and Hamilton's wrath was implacable.

A little later he, Hamilton, traveled through the North with a view to finding some other Federalist as strong with the mass of the party as Adams, but had to report reluctantly to his followers that no such man could be found. Accordingly, Adams and Pinckney again formed the Federalist ticket. It was not long before Hamilton revealed to his allies that he had written an elaborate letter, attacking Adams savagely, declaring him neither wise, safe nor honest as President, and giving at length with bitter emphasis his reasons for saying so. And then, after liaving, as he thought, proved by these reasons that Adams was grossly unfit to be President, he wound up by urging all Federalists to return him a second time to the high place for which he was so proven unfit. And he insisted that because he closed with this obviously reluctant recommendation he was not opposing Adams' reelection, a most grotesque bit of political lunacy.

He had this amazing letter in print, but had not sent it out when he showed it to some of his allies. Most of them saw its danger and the astounding foolishness—or worse—of sending it out, but the most that he would concede to their frightened remonstrance was that he would "distribute it privately and discreetly." Of course he might as well have talked of "discreetly" throwing coals of fire into a powder magazine. To suppose that he did not see this would be to "write him down an ass," and nobody ever did that.

He never had a chance to display this wonderful brand of discretion. Jefferson and Aaron Burr were the two opposition candidates, and somehow, nobody ever explained just how, while Hamilton's friends were urging him to destroy the few copies of the letter he had had printed and "take his medicine" like a man, and a good party man, one of these copies came into the possession of Burr, and at once red coals of fire were in the gunpowder. Whether it was the culpable carelessness or the treachery of Hamilton's printer, or of himself --- and at this day it looks as if it must have been one or the other— the mischief was done. Burr scattered the amazing letter of the Federalist dictator broadcast over the Union and the Federal party was demoralized. Four years later, when Burr had engineered some kind of fusion with many Federalists by which he was to be made Governor of New York, Hamilton defeated him, in favor of Morgan Lewis, by his own personal exertions among the Federalists inclined to the fusion, but though Hamilton's tactics did not this time involve the treachery involved in his treatment of Adams, Burr, unlike Adams, did not content himself with hatred, of and contempt for his enemy. In the fashion of the South at that time he forced a quarrel on Hamilton, ostensibly for other causes, challenged him, and as all the world knows, shot him fatally in July, 1804, thereby killing himself, indeed, politically, but revenging himself on his personal and political enemy.

Notwithstanding this demoralizing treachery of the Federalist party leader on the eve of the election, Jefferson and

Burr secured but seventythree electoral votes each—thereby forcing the House of Representatives to choose the President from the two—against sixty-five votes for Adams, and sixty-four for Pinckney, one Rhode Island elector voting for John Jay instead of Pinckney. Had New York voted as it had voted at the previous elections, and that it did not was probably due to Hamilton's blundering treachery, even more than to Burr's superior astuteness, or even bad Maryland divided its vote, as it probably would have done but for the disturbing influence of the Hamilton letter in Burr's hands, it is certain in the one case, and very far more than probable in the other, that Adams would have been given his second term, as his long and pre-eminent public services (notwith-standing all his infirmities of personal temper) richly deserved, as it is easy to see now.

CHAPTER III

The Monticello Dynasty

During the sitting of the Constitutional convention, and nearly all the time when the people were consciously preparing for it, Jefferson had been absent representing the Confederation at the French Court. While there he was in warm sympathy with the men who were active in bringing on the great revolution, and came home full of their theories. It seems strange now that he did not see that some of these theories, whether wholesome for the French or not, were certainly not wholesome for America. It seems even more strange that he did not see that America owed little gratitude to the French government for its aid in the American revolution, since he could hardly fail to know that aid would never have been given but for the sake of damaging England, France's hereditary foe. It is less strange, perhaps, that he did not see that such gratitude as Americans did owe for French aid was not due to the Frenchmen who soon rose to power and made the French revolution what it was during and after "the Terror," for before that time he had returned home.

But his sympathy with French theories put him at once in accord with the individualist Americans who dreaded everything that looked toward a "strong central government" as calculated to lead toward monarchism. He accordingly accepted the Constitution which he found in force on his return with great distrust and affiliated at once with those of his countrymen who had opposed it though he became Washington's Secretary of State and was long held in check by his force of character.

It is to the honor of his patriotism and his statesmanlike foresight that in one of the early acts of his administration, the Louisiana Purchase, he turned his back squarely on the particularism he had professed and practised and was able to carry his party with him, notwithstanding its "strict construction" principles. Patriotic as was the act, it throws an unpleasing light on his tendency to shiftiness as a party leader.

He did affect not a little of the "simplicity" in manner of which so much clap-trap has been written, but not to the extent of riding alone to the Capitol, hitching his horse to the fence and going alone before the Chief Justice to take the oath of office, according to the long popular story. As a matter of fact he had been, while Vice President under Adams, living in a boarding house on New Jersey avenue, in Washington, and on the morning of his inauguration he was escorted from that house, walking between two members of the outgoing Adams' Cabinet, by a battalion of infantry, while a "salute of honor" was fired by a battery of artillery in near by Alexandria. And when it is added that the oath was administered by Chief Justice John Marshall in the presence of a distinguished company at the door of the Capitol, one wing of which was then completed, we may be very sure that the ceremony lacked none of the impressive solemnity and dignity that could be given to it by men in that time and place.

That much of his "simplicity" was affected is fairly proved by the fact that prior to his setting out to build up a party on "strict construction," not only while at the Court of France, but at home as well, he was rather conspicuously what our later age would call a "dude" in dress and manner. The proof is made virtually conclusive by the fact that before his second term of office was half over he had discarded his old red waist-coat and his other rusty clothes and dropped nearly all his off-hand crudities of manner about his office and his home, as some of his contemporaries did not fail to put on record. It is a curious commentary on "free government" that no President of the United States, from Washington to Roosevelt, has ever so systematically and completely, one might also say so arbitrarily, "had his own way" as did Jefferson, who had built his political success on the glorification of the common people as distinguished from those who were then known as the aristocratic classes. He had it conspicuously when he bought Louisiana, when he staved off every effort to furnish the country with a navy competent to defend its commerce when all Europe was at war and preying on America. He had it when he was permitted, almost without criticism, to refuse, when subpoenaed as a witness, to give testimony in the trial of Burr for treason. He had it when he even staved off on to the shoulders of his successor the war with Great Britain, which he had done so much to make inevitable by pigeon-holing, of his own will, the treaty with that power negotiated by his own especially deputed commissioners, James Monroe and William Pinkney.

But he never had it more conspicuously than when, after having himself enjoyed two terms as President, he dictated, virtually, not only who should be his own successor, but who should be that successor's successor. When his second term was nearing its end there were three conspicuous aspirants for the succession, all members of his own party—James Madison, James Monroe and De Witt Clinton. Down to that time, and, indeed, for some twenty or more years later, national party conventions were unknown and candidates were selected and named by a caucus of the party members of Congress. It was no secret at that time that Jefferson lost no opportunity—and probably made opportunities if none came in any case without it—to express his wish that Madison should be named to succeed him, and that Monroe should follow next after, using all his influence with the younger man, Monroe, to persuade him that he could afford to wait, while Madison could not. Beyond two successors he modestly declined to interfere, possibly, as one of Madison's biographers hints, because Clinton was a New Yorker and not a Virginian, a delicate application, indeed, of the theory of "State rights."

During all the campaign for the Constitutional convention and the session of the convention, in which he was one of the delegates from Virginia, and next to Washington the most conspicuous, and certainly the most active, Madison was a Federalist of Federalists—that is to say, he was wholly identified in word and act with the men who came afterward to be called Federalists. He and Hamilton were always acting together, and after the Constitution was framed they, with some valuable aid from John Jay, wrote that convincing series of arguments in favor of the instrument which is known as "The Federalist."

Narrowly defeated for one of the first Senators under the Constitution by the gerrymandering tactics of Patrick Henry, who was a bitter opponent of the Constitution, Madison was chosen a member of the first House of Representatives by his own district. Long afterward he declared that he declined a Cabinet appointment proffered to him by Washington, because he thought that in the House of Representatives he could be of far more service in defending the Constitution he had done so much to frame and put into force, from "trials of a new sort in the formation of new parties attaching adverse constructions to it," but as these new trials and new parties and adverse constructions were not known until a considerable time after he took his seat in Congress and at once took a leading part in organizing the government, it is somewhat difficult to understand how this could have been his chief motive.

Be that as it may, he was in harmony with Hamilton and the others of the soon-to-be-called Federal party in most of the work of organization, and he himself introduced the first actual business measure—a bill to raise revenue for the support of the government from duties on imports—in which measure he had the support of the same men, the soon-to-be Federalists. It was not until questions arose of paying the national debt to soldiers and to those who had bought their claims, and also of the nation assuming the debts of the States, and until it became plain, as he and others had seen in the Constitutional convention, that slavery threatened to become a disturbing element in fixing party lines ; and, most of all, not until he had again come into close relation with his old friend Jefferson, now filling the post of Secretary of State, it was not until then that Madison began to give plain indications of a leaning toward the party of the strict constructionists. The second Congress had scarcely well opened when his defection from the Federal party grew reasonably well assured to discerning politicians, and long before its close it could no longer be doubted by any. Henceforth he and Jefferson were politically inseparable, and in due time lie was named as that statesman's successor by the statesman himself, whose will the party calmly accepted, though Madison's electoral vote was forty short of that given to Jefferson four years earlier.

Jefferson had made it plain that he wished Madison to be his immediate successor, and that Monroe should succeed Madison, but he did not quite direct just how long either should hold office. Late in his first term Madison found him-self very much "cornered." For years both England and France had been heaping outrages on the new republic, and yet neither Jefferson, nor Madison after him, had ever been willing to prepare for the war that must come if America did not go back into bondage to Europe. Down to the last of February, 1812, Madison believed that war must be with France, and so wrote his minister in Paris. Nothing whatsoever had changed in the outside world, but on April 1 Madison sent a laconic message to Congress, recommending a general embargo. Primarily it was aimed at' England, with whom to stop commerce would most injure commercial New England. The young leaders of the President's party were Calhoun and Clay, and they had filled the whole party with the war fever. Clay was ready to fight either, or even both, but it was decided to begin with England.

Meantime Monroe and De Witt Clinton remained Madison's chief rivals, and each was keen for war, as, it was evident, was a decided majority of Congress, where the party caucus talked of the next President between warlike debates in the regular sittings. On June 1, 1812, Madison's former message having brought the embargo it asked, he sent in another message, urging a declaration of war against England, which was promptly made. Somewhere between those two dates the Congressional caucus nominated Madison for a second term. Within a few months Josiah Quincy, of Massachusetts, declared in open debate in Congress that the war declaration was one of the conditions of the nomination, and though the men who made the nomination heard Quincy's plain assertion, they did not deny it. Some of them did say, indeed, that there was "no bargain." Probably not. When a master issues an order that the servant obeys, it can hardly be termed a bargain.

Four years later the differences in the ranks of the strict constructionists, out of which, together with the disintegration of the Federal party, was soon to grow the Whig party, had be-gun, and Clinton, showing leanings in that way, was "side tracked" from the Presidential con-test by being made Governor of the great State of New York. William H. Crawford, of Georgia, a self-made, able and somewhat shifty politician, had risen to be Monroe's leading rival, and was probably favored by the majority of the Congressmen of the strict construction or Democratic-Republican party. But Jackson, the rising idol of the more Democratic element of the party, did not like him, and Madison, with the over-shadowing influence of Jefferson behind him, succeeded in postponing caucus action from time to time, till the influence of these three men, standing for the past, the present and the future of the party, won away from Crawford enough votes to give Monroe a majority of eleven in the caucus, and so carried into effect Jefferson's practical dictation of eight years before.

The acquisition of Florida, the Missouri compromise, then supposed to be a settlement for all time of the threatening slavery problem, gave Monroe's first term a show of brilliant success that went far to assure him a second nomination, and this was strengthened by the hopeless disintegration of the Federal party, while the new Whig party had not yet crystallized into any effective power. Monroe was therefore re-nominated with little trouble, and so fragmentary was the opposition that Monroe received every electoral vote save one, and that one elector is said to have cast his vote for another principally because he was unwilling that any other than Washington should have a unanimous vote. In a way, however, it was a prophetic vote. It was cast for John Quincy Adams.

CHAPTER IV

The Last Of The Old Guard

The narrow escape, in 1800, from having Aaron Burr for President, had brought about the Twelfth Amendment to the Constitution, requiring electors to vote for two men, one as President and one as Vice President. This precluded any peril such as that threatened by the tie vote in 1800 for Jefferson and Burr, who were the nominees of the same party. It was provided, also, that in the event that no candidate should secure a majority of the electoral college, then the House of Representatives should choose the President from the three on the list of candidates having the largest number of votes. Five elections—Jefferson's second, and all of those of Madison and Monroe—passed without any occasion for appeal to the latter provision of this amendment. After the Washington elections, a caucus system had grown up under which candidates were nominated by a meeting of the members of Congress of each party, meetings which, for two or three elections, were secret, Jefferson was early to use it, when he secured, in 179G, the concerted approval of his candidacy by all the Congressional members of his newly organized party, then undergoing the process at his hands of being made compact and effective by rigidly applied discipline.

The two terms of Monroe, 1817 to 1825, have been called "the era of good feeling," because the Federal party was rapidly dying and only the drilled party of Jefferson remained in the field. No question of importance had arisen on which men could divide into parties along lines of real political principle. In that sense it was a very peaceful time. But the absence of differences of principle made opportunity for personal politics, built on the ambitions of individual leaders, and when one burrows into the annals of the time and uncovers the acrimony, the unscrupulous selfishness, slander and general untruth bred by these personal ambitions, to speak of the politics of that time as marked by good feeling seems extravagant burlesque or biting irony. Monroe had a cabinet of five persons, and of these, three, John Quincy Adams, William H. Crawford and John C. Calhoun, were openly known to be candidates for the succession long before Monroe's second term was half over. Adams had been Secretary of State through both terms, and it had grown to be a kind of tradition that the Secretary of State was, in a sense, heir apparent. But Adams did nothing to promote his OW11 cause. When asked by one of his friends, as early as 1818, before Monroe's first term was half over, if he did not intend to do anything toward succeeding to Monroe, he admitted that he "stood in line," so to speak, and his candidacy was an understood fact, but that he would do absolutely nothing to assure it. He would not refuse the office,—on the contrary, to have it given to him would be gratifying as proof that his countrymen approved his past service,—but he positively would not ask any man even for his vote. And he never did. While his antagonists were "moving heaven and earth," Adams never so much as asked a man to support him. Austere and forbidding in manner, while really brimming over with passionate devotion to the right as he saw it, brave, tireless, intensely American in feeling, yet always wholly just and clear-sighted to-ward all the rest of the world, with repelling faults of temper and manner that shut him off from having or trying to have any personal following, Adams was, in many respects, the most extraordinary man who has ever filled the Presidential chair, not excepting even Washington. The first President, indeed, would not seek office, did not at all wish office, and always took it against his own inclination. But Adams was ambitious as well as patriotic. His whole life was spent in the public service, and he really desired to be made President, because he was hungry for his countrymen's approval, but not even for that evidence of approval would he unbend from his austerely Puritan conscience and dignity. Almost alone among our public men, he rigidly practiced as well as preached that "the office should seek the man, and not the man the office."

Crawford, Monroe's Secretary of the Treasury, had only narrowly missed winning the nomination over Monroe, and from the hour he entered the Cabinet lost no opportunity for promoting him-self to be Monroe's successor, and in the early part of the struggle Calhoun, the Secretary of War, was also a candidate, all working on personal grounds for lack of any grounds of principle or policy.

To these three candidates were soon added Clay and Jackson from outside the Cabinet, each of them pushing his own cause to the utmost of his ability in his own way, while Adams could not be induced by his own friends, nor provoked by those of either of the other candidates, to push his own cause in any way save by the rigid performance of his Cabinet duties according to the dictates of his unyielding, narrow Puritan conscience. Monroe was strictly neutral, possibly because, to borrow from a biographer of Madison, neither of the five was a Virginian.

The other four were all hostile to Adams, though Calhoun was soon eliminated from among them through somehow being induced to content himself with standing for the Vice Presidency. And so the campaign went on through the larger part of Monroe's second term, and when the electoral vote was counted, Jackson had 99 votes, Adams 84, Crawford 41, and Clay 37, while Calhoun was indubitably Vice President. The House of Representatives, therefore, had to choose the President from among the three highest, Jackson, Adams and Crawford, and Clay's great influence in Congress, it was plain, was likely to determine which of them it should be.

Just then was started, by somebody who later dodged responsibility for it, the famous "bargain and corruption" story that Adams had bought Clay's support by promising to him the post of Secretary of State. Adams treated the slander with profound contempt, but Clay was frantic with rage, publicly denouncing the author of the story as "an infamous dastard and liar," and finally fighting a duel about it with sour old John Randolph, of Roanoke. Probably nobody nowadays believes there was any truth in the story, while there are those who, from circumstances that became known sometime later, do suspect that there was some such scheme talked over, even if not tried, among some of Jackson's friends, but without Jackson's knowledge, with an eye to winning Clay's support for him.

It was not needed to spur Clay with any motive more than he already bad. For some months before the election Crawford had been a physical wreck. Stricken by paralysis, he could not write even his name, and could scarcely speak intelligibly. For Clay to help him into the Presidency would have been folly. So far as he, or any other, could see, it would be simply to make Calhoun President, virtually at once, and actually within some short period. Perforce, therefore, Clay had to choose between Adams and Jackson, and how he would choose was a foregone conclusion. He had no great fondness for Adams, rather disliked him, in fact, but he admired his ability and honesty, and it was already growing plain to discerning politicians that around Adams and himself was steadily gathering the nucleus of a new great party, a party that did gather about them—himself more especially because Adams never was much of a party man—and bore the name of the Whig party. Moreover, Clay hated all "military heroes," and Jackson especially, with a perfect hatred.

Therefore he gave his influence for Adams, though Jackson's friends claimed that he was entitled to it for the reason that he had the largest number of electoral votes, an inadmissible claim because, to admit it, would be to degrade the House of Representatives from an electing body to a mere board of canvassers. Moreover, in many states the electors had been chosen by the legislatures, and it was contended that in a fair count of the popular vote, eliminating allowance for slave population, Adams had really a plurality of the vote of the people, and if the House was to veil its own distinctly conferred electing power in deference to any other vote, it should be to the vote of the people, so counted, rather than that of the electors. Adams was, therefore, chosen President in the House by the votes of thirteen states, against seven for Jack-son and four for Crawford.

Strangely enough, as it looks to us, Adams was by no means satisfied. What he craved chiefly was approval by a clear majority of the whole people, and if, by declining the House election, he could have run the race over again against Jackson alone, he would have gladly done so. But here again, to so decline could only operate to make Calhoun President, and he chose the less of what seemed to him two evils.

By the time this campaign had begun it was urged, as was entirely just, that the nomination of candidates by a congressional caucus, was really to confide the selection of the President and Vice President to Congress, a method of selection which the framers of the Constitution had, after long and exhaustive debate in the convention, definitely rejected. Therefore the caucus system, which had fallen off in favor even in 1820, was not resorted to in 1824 by anybody except Crawford. His friends called a caucus in February of that year in the usual way, but of 258 members of Congress only 68 attended, and, though it nominated him, four or five even of the few present voted against him. Jackson, Adams and Clay were candidates, not by any nomination of any caucus, but by common consent. Accordingly, in 1828 no caucus was held, but the nominations were made by the state legislatures. Tennessee really led off by the nomination of Jack-son even before Adams was warm in his seat, though it was not formally made by the legislature until October, 1826. The opposition to Adams' administration was in full swing before he had really taken any steps in formulating a policy. It looks unfortunate at this day that in the face of the "bargain and corruption" story, Adams did make Clay his Secretary of State, but it demonstrates the deep contempt Adams felt for the calumny and its authors, and was thoroughly characteristic of his unflinching courage and his abiding faith in his own sense of right. Nor does Clay's acceptance now seem at all out of harmony with his lofty patriotism and his high ambition to be of service to his country. Doubtless if Adams had chosen some other Secretary the act would have been damned by his enemies as a virtual confession.

None the less, it gave the opposition a weapon which was used mercilessly and unceasingly. Adams' whole term of four years was trans-formed into an open campaign for 1828. It be-came a personal struggle between Jackson, a brilliant and successful soldier, who, with his friends, promised a total revolution in methods of administration,—and kept their promise, too, when the result gave them the chance,—and Adams, a stern, relentless Puritan who spared himself no more than he spared others,—who stubbornly re-fused to use the patronage of his office for any friend whomsoever,—who would not remove any-body from office except for ample cause,—who, so far as office went, stubbornly refused to make any kind of distinction between friend and foe, —who therefore made no party following, con-ciliated no enemies, rewarded no supporters and alienated, politically, everybody except the few whose convictions were-such that they would vote for him or anybody else of like convictions whom they believed to be equally sincere. Through his whole term he saw the battle for the succession, which he really wanted, going against him day by day, yet would not lift his hand to stern the tor-rent save only to move right on in the discharge of what his conscience approved as his official duty. As he frankly said, and did, before and during his first campaign, he coldly refused to do anything whatsoever merely, or even partially, to promote his chances of re-election. Stubborn — one is almost moved to say insanely stubborn —in his own conscious high rectitude of purpose and of act, he went down to defeat rather than swerve from the rigid line of life he had laid down. If men would accept him on those terms, it was well, and he would be glad. If they would not, it was well, also. There is nothing else quite like it in our political history, probably not in that of any other country.

Considering what the masses of men were then, and, indeed, are still, is there any reason for wonder that Jackson defeated him by 178 to 83 electoral votes'

CHAPTER V

A New Presidential Era

The election of 1824 marked the transition from the earlier methods of the Republic to methods of a nominally wider Democracy. In the older States voting was still hedged about with a goodly array of conditions and restrictions. Some of them required more or less intelligence, knowledge and educational training, and some had reference to the ownership of more or less property. There were others, also, but all of them had been fixed with a view to placing the political power in the hands of those best qualified by mental discipline to form intelligent opinions on political questions, and also those who had some stake in the community in the form of individual property, and who therefore must feel a saving sense of responsibility, even if sometimes they were without mental training or even average mental capacity.

Without doubt this tended in some minds to-ward an oligarchy of some kind, not so much in form as in essence, but there is not now any belief that there was the least basis of truth for the often expressed fears of the Jeffersonians that the Federalists, any of them, desired to convert the government into a monarchy. Probably some of the followers of Jefferson believed there was such danger, while others only pretended to believe so, yet both classes worked together to-ward that far wider individualism which Jefferson had imported when he came back from France, just before the breaking out of the great revolution in that country. There was just as decided and as strong Federalism in the South as ever there was in the North, until it was set aside by the keener interest in slavery; and the political atmosphere generated by that "peculiar institution" was just as oligarchic, to say the least of it, as any Federalism known to New York or Boston. It seems strange, indeed, that Jeffersonian Democracy had its origin among the descend-ants of the Cavaliers and other branches of British gentry, but it is not a whit more strange than that aristocratic Federalism reached its highest development in such men as John Adams and Josiah Quincy and Daniel Webster among that sturdy Democracy that sheltered the fugitive regicides and clings to "town meetings" and "select-men" even yet in this twentieth century.

Naturally enough the new Democracy flourished most in the new states. The pioneers who settled them—not merely the border men, rovers and Indian fighters who broke the way into the wilderness, but the "settlers" who, sheltered be-hind that fringe of skirmishers, really subdued it to civilization—these pioneers were rarely drawn from the classes in the older states regarded as privileged but almost always were of the more enterprising individuals of the humbler classes, ambitious to lift themselves to the envied plane above, and gifted with more or less ability to attain their desires.

What they did not see, and what the corresponding classes do not now see, is that their want of information and of the trained habit of individual thinking leads them into a kind of blind, unquestioning hero worship, into acquiescence in some one-man power, quite as strongly as the more cultured classes tended toward aristocratic combinations of various kinds. Among the latter, lines of cleavage are constantly developing in the nature of the case, while the less informed and consequently less independent thinkers naturally cling closer and longer to the leadership of any able man who once gains their confidence.

Jackson, himself originally among the most illiterate of the pioneers, but with natural abilities far above the general level, not at first ambitious of distinction to any conscious extent, but bold, aggressive, a born fighter, driven by a tremendous motive power of emotional attachment or hatred, and capable of taking on the surface polish of the cultured with whom he might come in contact, was peculiarly fitted for the leadership of such relatively primitive men. He was a little slow about assuming active leadership at first, but when defeated by Adams in 1824, he grasped it boldly at once and held it with relent-less grip to the day of his death. Indeed, the cynically disposed among his adversaries said that thousands of his adherents continued to "vote for Jackson" long after he was dead.

Jefferson is recorded as saying to one of his associates in office that as "Federalists seldom die and never resign," it was necessary to somewhat assist the course of nature in that regard. Yet he was rather chary of removing officers, though he did remove thirty-nine, while Washington and Monroe removed nine each, the elder Adams ten, Madison five—and three of these defaulters—and John Quincy Adams none at all except "for cause," and only two even for cause. But within a year after Jackson took office he had removed 730 from office directly, and as with these went their leading assistants, it is believed that these removals entailed more than two thousand changes In the civil service, nor was "the axe" altogether idle after that.

This is not a place to discuss the public measures favored or antagonized by Jackson during his two terms, though one may say in general that he was often in the right, and at least sometimes wrong, and nearly always he was able to carry his party with him, whether what he did or refused to do entirely pleased it at first or not But it is at least certain that this wholesale decapitation of political adversaries and rewarding of friends gave him a disciplined army of political retainers, nearly every man of which stood ready to carry out his leader's will. If any was not so ready he soon ceased to be of the army.

No President before him had so welded his party into a disciplined unit, no other had even dreamed of so decimating and crippling his opponents. Yet it is not just to charge him, as many have done, with having invented this kind of party tactics. That distinction, if such it be accounted, probably belongs, to Aaron Burr as much as to any one individual. At all events, Jackson found it ready made and in perfect working order, as it had been for quite a number of years, in the political or party management in New York and Pennsylvania. It was William, L. Marcy, then Senator from New York, who when Jackson nominated Van Buren for Minister to England in 1831, in the debate on confirming him—which, by the way, was not done—gave utterance to the cynical declaration that "to the victors belong the spoils."

Whether Jackson contemplated a second term when he took the first is not quite certain. He rather disclaimed it for a time, on the score of his age and physical weakness. He did not, as Crawford said of John Randolph, "claim to be dying for forty years," but lie had, some years before, given the same reason for indisposition to being made one of the Senators from Tennessee. His strength was always affected by a wound in his breast received in his duel with Charles Dickinson in 1806, while in his collision with Thomas H. Benton and his brother, Jesse Ben-ton, in 1813, lie received a bullet in his shoulder which was not removed till about the beginning of his second term as President.

It is entirely probable, therefore, that he was sincere in his early protestations, but, if so, he soon changed his mind. The rejection by the Senate of his nomination of Van Buren to the English mission roused him, as opposition always did, to decisive and persistent action. From that time he was firmly resolved that Van Buren must be made Vice President during his own second term, soon fairly assured, and should succeed next to the Presidential chair. To that end he spared no exertion and used every influence in his power. His will was carried out in both respects. Van Buren was made Vice President in 1832 and President in 1836. It has been said, but with how much of truth one can hardly be sure now, that he even emulated Jefferson and demanded that Benton should succeed Van Buren.

And now, for the first time, the national party convention came into existence. But here again those who have thought it an invention of Jack-son's, though a little knowledge of party history would have corrected the notion, were in error. There was a convention, a small one, of delegates from eleven States, in 1812, which nominated De Witt Clinton for President, but it made no impression on events. The anti-Mason party, if any, invented it, holding a convention in September, 1830, which called another to be held in Baltimore, September 26, 1831. This latter met at that time and place, with 112 delegates, and nominated William Wirt and Amos Ellmaker, hoping that the then new Whig party would adopt their nomination. But Clay would not consent, because the anti-Masonic party had nothing whatsoever on which to base a national party. Wirt himself was for Clay and tried to withdraw. The anti-Masons would not let him do so, and the whole movement went to pieces.

Jackson "bettered the instruction." He and the members of his "kitchen cabinet" studied the new device. Two of that "cabinet" induced the New Hampshire legislature, late in the spring of 1831, to propose a convention for the following spring. The Washington Globe, conducted by another of the aforesaid cabinet, "played up" the project strongly, and accordingly the convention was held in Baltimore in May,

1832, after the managers had taken time to study and profit by all the omissions or other mistakes of the anti-Masons' convention of September, 1831, and the Whig—or National-Republican—convention in December, 1831, by which Henry Clay and John Sergeant had been put in nomination.

Ostensibly the convention had been called chiefly to nominate Van Buren, but it had been so astutely managed by the unseen operators that it had secured what card players call "the drop" on all the other parties, and had out-trumped all of them with an "address to the people," really a glowing panegyric of Jackson's first administration, though it still had nearly a year to run. And this was practically the birth of the party "plat-form."

And then came a real, simon-pure "Hurrah for Jackson" campaign, given a tone of broader reasonableness, if one may so speak, by the insistence of Clay that his party must make the preservation of the United States Bank the leading aim and shibboleth of the struggle. It was a mistake in Clay. A financial policy or institution that has been in use for twenty or thirty years must be sustained, if at all, by reason, with a basis of facts. The "plain people" were then too much carried away by hero worship to give much attention to studying finance, and, unfortunately for the bank, it did not have all the facts and reason on its side. Jackson's electoral vote rose from 178 in 1828 to 219 in 1832, while Clay had but 47, although John Quincy Adams had been given 83 against Jackson at his first election.

But behind the bank and all other public questions lay the fact that Jackson had secret advisers who were among the shrewdest and most adroit politicians in our history as the persons making up the before-mentioned "kitchen cabinet." These men were, at first, William B. Lewis, one of Jackson's neighbors, who had married one of his (Jackson's) nieces; Amos Kendall, a far-seeing, rather slippery political strategist Duff Green, a resourceful Kentucky editor, and Isaac Hill, another editor, but from New Hampshire. In the first half of his term Jackson quarreled with Calhoun and, by consequence, with Green, and the latter's place in the "cabinet" was taken by Francis P. Blair, an old co-worker with Kendall, who had followed him on the Kentucky news-paper.

Of these men Lewis was the most disinterested. All he asked as the price of his staying in Washington, as Jackson implored him to do, was some small office that would furnish him a modest living without obliging him to do much work, and that was all he ever had. He, more than any other. originated and set in motion most of those "spontaneous popular movements," beginning in un-likely places, but growing like a rolling snowball, that were so noticeable in our early political history, and nothing was too trifling for him to give it his best care. He never abated his zeal, either, though he must have seen very soon that Kendall had more selfish ends in view. These were the men who largely planned Jackson's political campaigns and largely directed the strategy and tactics. Lewis especially knew Jackson thoroughly, and when it was wise to speak to him and when it was better to keep silence. Other Presidents have had friends, intimates, favorites, who were not known to the public as advisers, but no President ever had so far-seeing and adroit a corps, nor was any other quite so generally guided by them. General Eaton, his Secretary of War, whose wife was unpleasantly conspicuous in the administration, was a delegate to the convention of 1832. He was opposed to Van Buren, and said so. Lewis advised him in a friendly note, that he would better vote for Van Buren, "unless he was pre-pared to quarrel with the General." Significant phrase; he did not feel so "prepared."

The steadying of the bands of discipline in the party was never plainer than when the convention met to nominate Jackson's successor. Van Buren had been given a very large majority for Vice President in the convention of 1832, but now he was given every vote. Not a man in the party dared offer a word in contravention of the dictate of the chief. And when it came to the election Van Buren had a clear majority of 46 over all other candidates, while R. M. Johnson, nominated with him for Vice President, had but precisely half of the electoral vote and had to be chosen by the Senate.

It was a curious situation. The nation had been born of a stern and dignified "declaration" against the rule of one man, the king. Erected into a constitutional representative government, the author of that declaration, professing belief that the chosen representatives were slowly trans-forming it back into kingly one-man rule, had built up a great party on a theory of the largest possible liberty for each individual, more especially each one of the common people. And now, in one-third of a century, that party had developed over itself, and therefore over the people of which it was a majority, a "one-man rule" more rounded and complete than had ever been exercised over the original colonies by the British monarch.

CHAPTER VI

Fighting The "Money Power."

To him who tries to think clearly most of the rabid talk against what many call "the money power," in which men have indulged at intervals for many years, is nothing short of fantastic. They talk of it often as if it were a peculiar kind of incorporeal monster chewing up every one it can lay hold on. They seem to regard that to which they give this name as a new and especially vicious brand of devil, when in sober truth it is, if any-thing at all, the very same old devil that has dwelt with—or in—mankind from his birth. The only difference is that His Evil Majesty uses a different weapon to work his ends in an industrial civilization than he used under the "robber barons" of Feudalism, the age-long orgy of the pagan imperialism of Rome, or the fierce and narrow theocracy sometimes found in earlier and in later times.

In truth money, in itself, or wealth, or whatsoever name men may give the thing they mean, is as absolutely neuter—that is, neither good nor evil—as it is possible for any human thing to be. Wealth piled higher than the Eiffel tower would never inflict harm on anything unless evil men seize and put it to evil uses. It is the oppressor that makes the victim, not the tool he uses, whether that tool be a gun or money paid or mere brute muscle. If all men were honest the "money power" would be felt no more as an oppression than is the force of gravitation. Money itself is not good or evil, nor is the possession of it by any man. It is the use that possessor makes of it that may be evil. If men would content themselves with teaching those who are to come after them what uses of opportunity are evil, and then con-fine themselves to punishing the men who use opportunity of any kind for wrong doing, they would get along toward the aim and end of their being just as fast, at least, as now, and be far happier in the process.

The men of seventy years ago were no wiser in applying knowledge than we are. They had devised a great national bank and other banks, also. Then, because these institutions made business matters run more smoothly, the whole people, including the bankers, went panic-stricken with prosperity, or what they took for prosperity. Speculation in everything made people crazy. President Jackson, always inclined to kick any kind of block against which he might bruise his foot, began a war against the bank, assailing what he imagined to be the "money power" rather than against the uses men were making of this and all other banks. The result was a financial revulsion and commercial depression, going nearer to being universal in this than in any other from which we have suffered.

Van Buren was inaugurated March 4, 1837, and before he had been two months in office the storm broke with amazing fury. He had not anticipated such a tempest, probably because of the very multiplicity of his mental occupations. He even thought Benton a bit over frightened, because he said the danger was close. Yet when the storm came, and the people, as they always have done and probably always will do, saddled the whole blame on the government, he met the hurricane of wrath with superb courage and a sound and lucid common sense which no one of our Presidents has surpassed. Few, indeed, of the men of today have anything but admiration for his whole treatment of that disastrous time, yet, though as little blamable as any of his country-men, he had to bear the popular anger and suffer for the sins of other men. He might have out-grown some of the odium by the time of the next campaign, 1840, but for the fact that though there was a revival of business in 1838, there was also a relapse into bank failures and unreasoning fear in 1839, followed by more prolonged and discouraging debility than before, and so lie had to go into the conflict of 1840 bearing this double bur-den. It is easy now to see his steady courage and strong, clear sense. Even Von Hoist, chronic sore head as lie is, and who, therefore, often writes as if he felt that to praise anybody else must be to depreciate himself, accords him unqualified praise in this case.

This burden of blame for a double distilled panic

probably would have been, by itself, enough to defeat the administration, but it had to bear several other burdens. In 1838 there was a rebellion in Canada, with which there was much sympathy in the more northern parts of New York and New England and much use of our territory by the rebels. Van Buren maintained our honorable and legal obligations toward Great Britain with firmness and dignity, and his attitude therein lost him New York in 1840, when, but for that reason, state pride in her own citizen probably would have given him its vote despite the panic.

During his term, too, the old boundary dispute between Maine and the British province of New Brunswick broke out into dangerous disorders, and here, again, he displayed a high sense of honor and a statesmanlike moderation and dignity which the "hardy lumbermen" of Maine so resented that it lost him that state also.

In the South, too, slavery had fomented disaffection even toward Jackson, which had bred factional revolt against him, led by Hugh L. White, the real motive power of which was the Southern resolve to annex Texas. Van Buren had opposed annexation and never could be induced to favor it. The most he could be induced to say was that while still opposed to it, he would yield if a Congress chosen especially on that issue should legislate for it, and he would not, or did not, say even this until 1844. So into the campaign of 1840 he went handicapped by the panic of 1837, for which he was' in no way responsible and which he had met with sound sense and courage, by his coolness and firmness toward Canadian rebellion, by the ultra-jingo accusation of truckling to

England in the Northeastern boundary dispute, and by his known hostility to the Texas annexation scheme.

The Whig party, on the other hand, went into it with a wild yell for a successful soldier. It threw overboard Clay, who, more than any other man, had made the party, nominated for Vice President Tyler, a renegade Democrat who favored annexation, refused to make any declaration of principles or platform, but rang the changes on the "hard times," falsely attributed to the Van Buren administration; made a rallying cu of "Two dollars a day and roast beef" for every workingman, and out shined the most rabid Jeffersonian in adulation of "the common people." The whole nation was stirred to a crazy and violent enthusiasm. There were huge mass meetings on the battlefield of Tippecanoe and in all other parts of the country, especially the West and South. There were barbecues innumerable and "hard cider" galore, free to all—save the managers who furnished it. There were gray-beard processions of "revolutionary soldiers," many of them pretended, but many also real. Women and children, who knew nothing of the issues or of the campaign save its excitement, turned out in hysterical shoals not unlike those that have been used in the anti-liquor campaigns of the past year or two. Log cabins, supposed to be like that of Harrison, where he had told his soldiers they would be sure to find "the latch-string always hanging out" for them, were carried on wheels all over the country, with coon skins nailed to the sham logs, live raccoons tied to the roofs and a barrel of cider on the tail of the wagon, and rosy-cheeked country girls with gourds serving out its contents—not always clear cider, either—to all comers. Song writers blossomed out in more doggerel songs than have been known in all other Presidential campaigns before or since. Van Buren, who, with all his faults, history now declares one of our ablest, most far-seeing and patriotic Presidents, was drenched with an overwhelming torrent of blackguard ridicule. The whole campaign degenerated into a crazy orgy—a kind of crude, semi-barbaric, bastard mardi-gras, rooted in a sham of baseless faith in political negation, into which even the solemn and stately Webster—his great rival, Clay, he thought had been "shelved"—was swept as by a whirlwind and mouthed flamboyant rhetoric from every stump lie could reach.

Of all the free states Illinois alone was carried by Van Buren, and of the thirteen slave states he carried but five, the other eight giving majorities for Harrison. The popular vote swelled suddenly. from about a million and a half in 1836 to nearly two and a half millions in 1840, though it grew only by 300,000 between 1840 and 1844. The most utterly and grotesquely senseless, unmeaning and ridiculous campaign the country had ever known, or, for that matter, has ever since known, drew out, therefore, a larger percentage of the possible voters than any other. There is nothing else in our history of which we ought to be so thoroughly ashamed.

A month after his inauguration Harrison, pathetic old victim of a foolish popular madness, died, and within a few months Tyler, as the men who nominated him might have known he would do, vetoed two bills for a National bank successively passed by Congress, the "independent treasury" law, a monument to Van Buren's sound financial sense and sagacity, which he had succeeded in having enacted only a year before, was repealed and was not revived for five years.

Four years later the Whigs, sore and humiliated over the defeat which their insincere policy in 1840 brought on them, embodied in Tyler, turned back to Clay, whom they could have elected, perhaps, in 1840, save that between him and Van Buren there was no choice on the annexation of Texas, since both opposed it. In the Democratic convention of 1844 a majority of the delegates had been "instructed" for Van Buren, but the Southern leaders of the party were bent on annexation and set about either forcing him to declare him-self for annexation or evading their instructions. They had secured from Jackson in 1843 a letter strongly urging annexation. It was made public in March, 1844, and a Southern delegate wrote to Van Buren asking squarely how he stood. He coveted the nomination deeply, but he would not "stultify his past." He replied that his administration had, in 1837, refused the offer of Texas for annexation, and his views had not changed. The most he would concede was, as before stated, that he would yield his own personal opposition to the expressed will, should such be made known by legislation, of a Congress elected with direct reference to that question. That straightforward reply sealed his fate.

In the Democratic convention of 1840 the " two-thirds rule" had not been adopted. Now the Southern delegates insisted that it be revived and they won over Northern delegates enough to adopt it by 148 for it to 118 against it, a vote carried not without violent disorder. Then the balloting began and, on the first ballot Van Buren was given 146 votes, a clear majority of the convention of thirteen votes. The instructed dele-gates had technically "obeyed their instructions," but on the next ballot his vote fell to seven or eight less than a majority, and after more violence and disorder and a narrow escape from declaring Van Buren nominated as the choice of a majority, the South carried its point by the nomination of Polk, a man of more ability than he has been credited with, but who had no "claim" to the place in a genuine party sense and who had come before the convention solely because the choice of his own state, Tennessee, for Vice President.

The convention was shrewd enough to couple with the demand for the "re-annexation," it was called, of Texas a demand for "the whole of Oregon," out of which grew the famous party cry of "fifty-four, forty or fight." The subsequent course of the negotiations showed clearly enough that they, the Southern delegates, were not sincere in this demand, for before Polk's term was over the present boundary of 49 degrees north in-stead of 54 degrees 40 minutes was accepted. Oregon could not be made a slave state. It was, however, "a good enough Morgan till after the election" in Thurlow Weed's cynical phrase about another matter, and it won for Polk not a few Northern votes that otherwise would -have gone to Clay.

Both parties attempted something like the whirlwind style of the campaign of 1840. All over the land there were flamboyant raising of party flag poles, the Whigs using ash because Clay's Kentucky home was called "Ashland," the Democrats choosing hickory, from Jackson's pet sobriquet of "Old Hickory." They did their best to make it another "Jackson campaign," Polk only being supposed to carry out his will. Except for the Harrison break of 1840, the "Jackson dynasty" was thus made to run from 1828 to 1848.

There were again great barbecues, mass meetings, one immense one attended by people from hundreds of miles away despite the difficulties of travel, held on the grounds of "The Hermitage," Jackson's Tennessee home, where the old dicta-tor stood almost literally "with one foot in the grave." There were huge processions with great "floats" of many kinds, some loaded with pyramids of young country girls in white, one for each state in the Union. Now and then there were a few belated "hard cider and coon skin" roisterers surviving from 1840. There were long, straggling ranks of banner-carrying little boys called "Hickory Buds"—the writer hereof was one of them—wrestling with flapping banners in wind and dust.

There was what seemed to youngsters a vast deal of enthusiasm and noisy patriotism, but as one looks back upon it now, it lacked spontaneity. It was mainly "pumped up." .The old issues had passed away, and even a boy could see that through the dust and clamor about Texas and Oregon there loomed some yet shapeless shadow of something sterner and more grim standing close behind the ever receding curtain that hides the future. The frowning specter of the slavery struggle had fairly entered the verge of party politics.

CHAPTER VII

The Gathering Of The Storm

When Van Buren went before the Democratic National Convention of 1844 he, both constructively and in terms, pledged himself to abide by its action and support whomsoever it might nominate. He knew when he did so that a majority of the convention would be for himself, and doubt-less he had reason to hope that that majority would carry out the will of the party broadly ex-pressed in "instructions" by those who sent them. As an honorable party man he had no reason to suspect that his opponents within the party would keep only the letter and violate the spirit of their own implied or expressed pledges as party men. Yet they so acted, using his own majority to make a rule which they knew would defeat him, thereby evading the instructions under which alone they held their places, and by this nefarious juggle cheated him out of the place to which he was fairly entitled.

He did not, however, as some other men have done, regard their perfidy as justifying him in repudiating his own pledges. He had a wider sense of party honor. He kept his promise, supported Polk himself, and urged his friends to do so. He even prevailed on his friend Silas Wright, one of the most brilliant and popular Democrats of the day (who had indignantly refused the convention's nomination for Vice President on the ticket with Polk), to accept the Democratic nomination for Governor of New York. Had Wright held to his purpose to decline that nomination also, as he would have done but for Van Buren's persuasion to do otherwise, the history of the country would quite surely have been very different from what it has been. For, though Wright was himself elected by a majority of some 10,000, not even his candidacy, joined with Van Buren's urgent sup-port of Polk, could avail to give the state to Polk by even half the majority given to Wright. Polk, however, did carry the state by about 5,000 majority, and the electoral vote of that state made him President. Even as it was, the vote for James G. Birney, the candidate of the Liberty party--soon to be -mown as the Free Soil party—who had been the candidate of that party in 1840 also, rose from about 7,000 in the whole country in that year to 62,300 in 1844. In New York alone the Birney vote of 1844 was some 16,000, and as all the Liberty party men were opposed to annexing Texas, as was Clay also, while Polk was running solely because he favored it, the strong probability is that but for the irritation growing out of the Van Buren affair quite half the Birney vote in New York would have been given to Clay, and that would have made him President. In that case Texas would not have been annexed when it was at least ; we would have had no war with Mexico, and our own Civil Wdr would probably have been postponed twenty or thirty years, though it was inevitable in some shape sooner or later.

Thurlow Weed, one of the most astute and resourceful of the many adroit political manipulators developed by our party politics, records in his autobiography that in the spring of 1846, within a month after General Taylor's two defeats of the Mexican forces near the Rio Grande River, he went by steamboat from Albany to New York. On the boat, quite by accident, he met Colonel Joseph P. Taylor, of the United States Army, a younger brother of the then newly famous General. Weed was "playing politics" always, awake and asleep, apparently. In his invariable way he asked Colonel Taylor about his brother's politics. The reply was that the General "had no politics," cared nothing about politics or party, and rarely ever voted. But, said the brother, he "has some very strong prejudices," he was, for example, a warm admirer of Clay, had always disliked General Jackson—then only a few months dead—and was so prejudiced against foreign manufactures that he would not wear a coat the materials of which, even to the buttons, were not of domestic manufacture. Upon this Weed shrewdly remarked that these prejudices were probably quite as important as principles. The brother asked why he was so curious about it, and Weed replied, "Be-cause, if your brother finishes this war as he has begun it, he will be the next President of the United States."

The brother laughed at this as absurd, but soon thought

differently, and this began a correspondence between him and Weed, of which General Taylor was kept advised, and which Weed prosecuted assiduously. Within a month— that is, in June, 1846, Weed published a paragraph in the Albany Evening Journal, which he then controlled, in which, adverting to the election of Generals Jackson and Harrison to the Presidency, lie said that General Taylor was already "in the minds and hearts of many for the same high place, and one or two more successful battles would carry him there in 1848." And then and there the Presidential campaign of 1848 was really begun.

Weed claims that he spared no efforts during the succeeding two years to promote Taylor's nomination, finding it often an "uphill job." Clay and Webster were both eager aspirants. Clay thought himself fully entitled to it by reason of his narrow miss of election in 1844, and Weed admits that he was unquestionably the first choice of three-fourths of the Whigs of New York, and probably of a large majority of them in the whole country. Webster no doubt felt that Clay had been given his chance and had failed, while he himself had never been given a chance. Weed virtually concedes justice in the claims of both these eminent men, but stubbornly stuck to Taylor because) he says, lie felt sure that if the Whigs should not nominate him in their convention the Democrats would be sure to take him up and elect him. It seems a strange reason, indeed, for a political party to nominate a man because its opponents want him. It eliminates wholly from party management all question of principle or even of administrative policy.

Taylor himself said that he had been approached on the

subject by representatives of both par-ties, but it is a little hard to see why Weed should have feared, at least in the latter half of his campaign, that if the Whigs wouldn't the Democrats would, seeing that it was known long in advance of the time of the conventions that the Democratic convention would be held in May and that of the Whigs a month later. If the Democrats had any such notion they therefore had the opportunity. Possibly Weed felt that lie had gone too far to retract before he knew the convention dates, but far more likely is it that the whole Taylor movement, in Weed and others also, was purely and simply a case of subserviency to mere "availability," and that, too, based wholly on the glamor of fame surrounding the successful soldier. The Democrats tried it with Jackson and won. The Whigs tried it with Harrison and won. They now tried it with Taylor, and won, and strangely enough, death robbed them, once of all and once of more than half, of the fruits of victory in both cases. They tried it once more in later years and suffered the most inglorious of all their defeats.

During Polk's term Texas had been annexed, with conditions securing for slavery at once two new Senators and the possibility of eight more whenever needed, and the war with Mexico had been fought, bringing more territory for slavery but how these Southern gains should be enforced had not been decided upon before the campaign of 1848 was at hand. Nine-tenths of the Northern Democrats were hostile to slavery at heart, but they recognized the fact that it had existence in the old states by inherited law, and in a few new ones by the voluntary action of their own people. Morally it was indefensible, but politically they had no right to interfere.

They would fight rather than it should be imposed on themselves, but the southern people had precisely the same legal right to keep it that the northern people had to refuse it, and furthermore, for all the ends for which governments are instituted among men, they regarded this Union of States as of far higher value than the whole black race.

It was the fatal mistake of the Southern leaders that they did not understand this attitude, and they were surprised at the evident increase of Northern willingness to translate a hitherto latent hostility toward slavery into action, when the time came to frame governments for these new acquisitions. The Senate would "organize" no territory with any provision hostile to slavery. The House of Representatives would listen to no bill for organization without it prohibited slavery as clearly as the "Ordinance of 1787" did for the Northwest Territory.

For the time there was no other question of principle or policy for parties to differ about, and on this there was what seemed to be a hopeless deadlock between the two houses of Congress, and this was the condition when the party conventions met in 1848. The Democratic convention repeated the old platform of 1840, adding resolves about slavery which amounted to deprecating all party debate about it, and then nominated General Lewis Cass, who practically added to the platform his famous Nicholson letter, in which lie laid down very clearly the doctrine that the people of each Territory should be permitted to settle for themselves the question of slavery or no slavery. This is essentially the popular sovereignty which the world has generally charged Stephen A. Douglas with having invented in 1854.

The Whigs repeated their old plan, made no platform at all, and took up General Taylor, for the same "reasons" that had moved them to take up General Harrison eight years before. Nominally the result was the same, the election of the soldier but, while the victory of 1840 was the fruit of a popular furor, that of 1848 was not at all floated by any wave of enthusiasm, but was purely a matter of shrewd party warfare, though beyond question behind the tactics of those who made the result certain there was honest political conviction, and moral conviction also behind that.

Van Buren had always been hostile to slavery and resolute to confine it where the formation of the government found it, and to resist all attempts to extend it into any territory where it had not thus existed. He had never made any secret of his sentiments in that regard. Men could hold opinions on slavery either way, and yet be good Democrats, with more consistency than they could be good Christians. He had been given the nomination for his second term in 1840, and had been deprived of the fruits of it by a kind of accident, as truly an uncontrollable accident as is a stampede of half wild cattle. He had asked, and no open objection had been made, to be given another chance in 1844, and no other Democrat could advance any party claim at all approximate, yet he had been cheated of what he had every right to expect by as mean and treacherous a juggle as any party managers could be guilty of. He had kept faith to his pledges in that campaign with strict honor. Now he was free to act in strict accord with his convictions.

The Free Soil party gave him its nomination, and to Charles Francis Adams, the son of his old antagonist, John

Quincy Adams, its nomination for Vice President. He could not have any anticipation of being elected, but his party polled nearly 300,000 votes, of which more than 120,000 were cast in his State, New York, or 6,000 more than were cast for Cass.

The great body of the people were bewildered or appalled by the growing arrogance of the slave-holders' demands. They had tried, and still tried, to exclude slavery from party politics, and, largely out of habit, most of them still voted the " regular" tickets. The Whigs tried to infuse some-thing of the furor of 1840 into the campaign, and the Democrats tried also, but just as like efforts had been only half-hearted in 1844 they were less than half-hearted now. There was general lassitude. The whole campaign of the "great parties" was perfunctory and formal. Most men shrank with aversion from discussing the new question which they all knew in their hearts was the only one in which there was any vitality.

The only approach to earnest enthusiasm was shown by those who had boldly broken old party ties, and their 300,000 votes for Van Buren and Adams made up the controlling factor in the election, though they did not choose an elector, and Taylor became President by a minority vote of the people, his renown as soldier giving him a small plurality over Cass, so distributed as to give him an electoral majority of 36. And then the hot and weary combatants sat down to breathe, with a quaking dread of what might happen upon the re-assembling of Congress.

CHAPTER IIX

The Approach Of The Storm

General Taylor was a Southern slave holder, but lie was a tolerable Whig and, before all, he was a citizen of the United States, the nation, and all his active life had been spent in its service. The whole people were breathless with suspense as to what would be done with the problems, complicated with slavery, precipitated on us by the new territory acquired with Texas and from Mexico. The great battle opened in Congress with Taylor's recommendation of the admission to the Union of California as a free state, as her people provided in the Constitution they had framed. Out of the many sided discussions then arising grew the celebrated "compromise measures of 1850," which Clay sought to have enacted in one capacious law. Congress would not accept them as a whole, though the several measures, which need not be enumerated here, were severally adopted by varying majorities, some of them very narrowly.

Had General Taylor lived, probably not one of them, perhaps not even the admission of California, could have been passed. The threats of disunion which had been more or less brandished, sometimes in earnest and sometimes in empty "bluffing," from the very formation of the government, by more or less disgruntled people North as well as South, had aroused the stern old soldier's wrath, and he declared with grim emphasis, "Disunion is treason." But the man who had borne the toils and hardships of war through forty years— war with Great Britain, with the then implacably warlike red men of all fighting tribes, with Mexican armies always with the odds against him, sometimes five to one, and had never been defeated—this man was broken down, not in spirit but in physical strength, by sixteen months of being President ; was stricken by illness on July 4, 1850, and died five days later, in the very midst of the struggle over the proposed compromise, opposing it to the last.

This elevated Fillmore to the Presidency—a man of fine ability and very high personal character, but with such mental nerves that, if we had bestowed names after the fashion of the red men, he might have been called "Man-Afraid-of-the-Fire-Eaters." Webster, Corwin and other nervous men came into the Cabinet, and the whole influence of the administration, which Taylor had thrown against the compromise measures, was now arrayed in their favor, and in September, 1850, they separately became laws, one of them that incendiary firebrand, the Fugitive Slave law.

There is no doubt that an immense majority of the people looked upon the adoption of these measures as a final settlement, so far as party politics could be affected, of the dangerous slavery question: After the settlement effected by the Missouri Compromise, in 1820-21, this prickly theme seemed to sleep for some fifteen years. Now and then some relatively small thing served to warn that it was only sleeping, not dead, but there was nothing like a broad and real awakening until the Texas annexation movement was begun, about 1835. Van Buren thought he killed that movement when he refused the offer of the Texan rulers and people to join our Federal Union in 1837, while in truth it killed him, politically. New territory had revived the old questions of 1820, but now these had been settled for every square foot of ground the country owned.

Beyond all doubt the mass of the people were more than tired of the slavery agitation. It had consumed the time of legislators to the serious detriment of other legislation very greatly needed; it had very gravely injured business prosperity and more greatly endangered the public peace. Few were entirely content with all the conditions of the adjustment, but they were weary of discord and glad to welcome peace.

This was apparent on the surface and especially in the election of 1852. The nominations made that year by the two parties had not been expected. There were many conspicuous men among the Democrats. Buchanan, Cass, Douglas and Marcy were the chief competitors, but there were several others voted for in the convention, and when, after forty-eight vain ballots, the choice fell in the forty-ninth to Franklin Pierce, of New Hampshire, it was commonly supposed that it was another case of mere "availability," resorted to largely because it was feared that the struggle among the leaders would result in bitterness that might affect the party strength at the polls. But it is more probable that the real, though not avowed, reason why the convention gravitated to Pierce was his attitude toward slavery as related to political action, which was well known to the Southern leaders, but not at all to the general public. Pierce was a man of strong native ability, hardly in the first rank with such as Webster, perhaps, but of much higher and wider intellectual culture than many men far better known as states-men. He had been a Senator from his state for five years, but resigned in the middle of the Tyler administration, and thereafter had refused offers of other places of distinction. Not even Van Buren had been more distinguished for mingled dignity and puavity of manner, the poise, polish, ease and elegance of the mostly highly cultivated social rank. Nor was there ever any question, as there was sometimes in Van Buren's case, of his entire sincerity of political conviction. He had preferred to devote himself to his profession, but Southern leaders knew that in his view the political aspect of slavery, the so-called "compromises of the Constitution," should be paramount in the attitude toward it of every American states-man. That knowledge was what gave him the nomination.

Like the Democrats, the Whigs declared the compromise measures of 1850 to be a "finality" in the matter of slavery agitation, a mandate that it "must be removed from politics." Like them, too, they had many aspirants for the nomination, among them being Clay, Webster, Fillmore, who eagerly sought the place; Clayton, who had been Taylor's Secretary of State; General Winfield Scott, who had been trying for years to "break into politics," and whose appetite for political distinction had been sharpened anew by Taylor's success, not to speak of others. It took more ballots for them to make a choice, but after fifty-two trials, tempted by recollection of having twice succeeded with military heroes, they settled upon General Scott.

Strenuous efforts had healed for a time the schism in the Democratic party in New York, and nothing in the campaign was more significant of how real and widespread was the popular hope that slavery had been actually "removed from politics" by the "finality" of 1850 than the fact that, though the Free Sailors kept up their organization and made a nomination, their vote in 1852 fell off from close to 300,000 in 1848 to a little more than 166,000, or nearly one-half. It is interesting to observe, too, in passing, that, though Pierce was given 254 electoral votes out of a total of 296, or a majority more than six times larger than General Scott's whole electoral vote, yet his majority in the popular vote was only 48,747 in a total vote of 3,154,201.

There was a ground swell, so to speak, in the public feeling, as there often is in the ocean when the storm is past and the sun again is shining and the winds are still, but for a time it was not great. Considering how fierce had been the excitement in the summer of 1850; that Clay had pleaded with tears for his compromise; that Texas was then actually mobilizing a military force to wrest from the possession of the United States a portion of New Mexico which she (Texas) claimed to be hers, and other states were preparing to back up Texas in her claim; that the grim old soldier then in the

White House had sent an order to the officer commanding the United States forces in New Mexico to move forward to the boundary line and suffer no hostile foot to cross it, from Texas or any-where else—considering all the conditions, the dis-quiet was hardly as great as might have been expected.

The political ground swell showed itself most frequently for nearly two years in little bursts of heated argument in private life, and in the growing caustic criticism by the more clear-sighted anti-slavery men, of the drastic Fugitive Slave law, which made part of the so-called pacification of 1850. In the active closing months of the campaign itself it was often rather amusingly notice-able how "hard up" the speakers were for materials of which to weave appeals. Occasionally one or another among them would momentarily forget the pacification and touch on some of the yet smoking fires of 1836 to 1850, and in a flash would begin to bristle, while his hearers would glance at each other with uneasy smiles. But this would be by force of habit, and the ready stump speaker usually made use of the inadvertence to lead to congratulations that those lamentable days were happily gone, "as we all hope, forever."

There was practically no difference between the two great parties on any subject that had any present life. For a long time slavery had so dwarfed every other theme and honey-combed both parties that men almost forgot why they were called Whigs or Democrats; and stump speakers eagerly went back from the argument of grave questions to the trivial balderdash of personality. No little fun of a very acrid flavor was poked at each of the leading candidates. "Old Fuss and Feathers," a nickname fastened long before on Scott because of his fondness for personal display as an officer, was dragged out of the dust bins of memory and the changes rung on it to weariness. As if, provided a man is a good soldier in other respects, it matters anything at all whether he goes into battle bedizened like Murat or shirtless as mythical King Dagobert. So, also, the old soldier was laughed at for his rhetoric about the "hasty plate of soup" and his maladroit glorification of "that rich Irish brogue," for the vain old man was inclined to be as flamboyant in his phrasing as he was in but-tons and gold lace and floating plumes.

It was rather difficult to find ways of ridiculing Pierce. Manifestly one cannot be sure that want of reputation necessarily implies want of ability, and nobody will claim that every man must of necessity be all he is reputed to be. There was not much material for lampooning in the facts that a man serves five years in the United States Senate, the youngest member in it, and then re-signs with the respect of his colleagues because he prefers private life to public life ; that he de-clines an offer of a seat in the Cabinet of a national President; that he refuses a nomination, when it is equivalent to election, to be governor of his state ; that he volunteers as a private soldier in his country's forces for a foreign war, and is soon elevated to be brigadier general, largely because conspicuous for quickness and capacity in soldierly qualities from his boyhood and his college years ; nor that almost his only, and certainly his closest and most intimate friend is his country's most distinguished author. But some-body did find out that when he insisted on going into battle at the head of his brigade when he should have been in a hospital bed, he had fallen unconscious from his horse, and then tried to sneer him down as a coward. The attempt re-acted in his favor, but all these things on both sides serve now to show how barren the campaign was in any matter for serious controversy, save only the one thing that both tried to feel was "finally settled" and resolutely tried to keep out of sight. The resolute determination to blink at what nearly all secretly felt to be inevitable, to "put off the evil day" as long as possible, made it a dull and spiritless campaign.

The most significant fact of the campaign, viewed as a struggle between organized political parties for the control of the policy of the national government, was the evidence it proffered of the death of the old Whig party as an organization. It had lived as such through nearly two decades, and twice during its life had lifted its candidate into the Presidential chair. Both of these men had been soldiers and not at all tried statesmen. Both died early, one of them very early, in their new service, and each was succeeded by a Vice President who refused to carry out the policy for which his chief had stood. It was a strange fatality to overtake a party, and it is easy to see why hasty opinion at the time saddled the blame for defeat on the man nominated by the party, its third soldier candidate. There was little sound reason for the opinion. So far as anyone could see then, so far, indeed, as one may fairly see now, there was as much ground for expecting ability of administration from General Scott, if elected, as there ever had been to expect it from either General Harrison or General Taylor. There may have been little in either case, but that was no explanation of the disastrous de-feat of Scott while both the others had succeeded. The real significance of the result in 1852 lay in the small increase of the aggregate vote over that of four years before. Such gain as there had been was nearly all for the Democratic party. It should have been seen more clearly than it was seen that there must have been an immense number of voters who were not content with either party, and that this must be because of the intrusion of some new question or interest.

It was inevitable that any new question would damage most that one of the old parties which was the less securely grounded on political principle. The Whig party had for its real informing inspiration the principle known as broad construction, which it had inherited from the old Federal party, but it was very chary of admitting the fact, and placed emphasis mainly on matters which were almost wholly of administrative policy. It was not an original, creative party in the same sense that the Democratic party was because admitting its heritage from the old Jeffersonian Republicans. They were strict constructionists in principle, but they did not hesitate to practice broad construction in acquiring Louisiana, Texas and the country conquered and bought from Mexico and from Spain, but, having acquired those do-mains, they insisted upon applying the "strict" principle to governing them, in the interest of slavery, out of which sprang the new question on which the Whig organization went to pieces.

So far as that party stood for anything vital in principle or, indeed, in administrative policy, it could not die while free institutions survived among men. But ignoring, almost as if ashamed of it, its real informing principle, and addressing itself almost wholly to matters of policy only, it was, as an organization, thrust aside when a new aspect of the old principle of human freedom arose for solution.

The old "strict" and "broad" principles are as vital today as they were a century ago, and the Republican party .is as much heir to the old "broad" principle of Federalism as ever the Whig party was, and is far more willing to admit and defend it, while it holds as firmly to the policy of protection. There were protectionists before the Whig party was organized. Jackson himself was one of them for a time. There was a United States bank before the Whig party was born and espoused that policy. There may be another be-fore the nation has run its course in history.

CHAPTER IX

The Storm Draws Nearer

If Jefferson had not invented the Democratic party, somebody else would have invented its equivalent. It was inevitable that any written constitution would give rise to differences of construction, generally divisible into two classes, the literal or strict and the liberal or broad. It was equally inevitable, in the nature of humanity, that each class or party, the "strict" and the "broad," would be sure, sooner or later, to find itself confronted with the necessity for choosing whether to forego doing something which it strongly desired to do or abandon for the time the school of construction it habitually avowed and observed.

Jefferson had the experience early. He had barely taken the Presidential chair to which his party of "strict" had elevated him, when he was face to face with the necessity for buying Louisiana, and he had no time to waste—he must " take it or leave it" at once. He was too able and clear sighted to hesitate about the act of buying. He bought without delay. But he knew that in so doing lie marched under the banner of the "broads." He did have the uneasiness of mind at the time to ask for an amendment of the Constitution which should "make an honest" states-man of him, so to speak, by reaching back and legitimizing his act; but when the people at large proved ready to adopt the result without any amendment, he was glad to accept the popular approval "with satisfaction," as he said. Ten years later, probably, he would not even have thought of asking for an amendment.

After Whitney's cotton gin had begun to show its marvelous effects on slave labor, Jefferson's party of "strict" was very ready, as regarded slavery, to follow his example in varying his practice from his preaching. It was ready to sacrifice to its "strict" scruples a goodly slice of Maine and a five hundred mile wide block of Oregon. But whenever it had a chance to extend the area of slavery, its theory on principles of construction expanded as promptly as steam. In such small matters as buying Louisiana, in buying Florida, in waging a costly war because of having annexed Texas, in the conquest and nominal buying of a third of Mexico, in the Gadsden purchase of more of Mexico, in the Platte purchase, Congress had, in "strict" Democratic opinion, abundant power under the Constitution; but when it came to preferring freedom over slavery in the territory it had bought or conquered, that body was, in its opinion, powerless. It might, so to speak, buy a farm, make all the family pay for it, and then give it to the uses of one alone.

In the Pierce election the "strict" had made both parties declare slavery forever settled and banished from politics. Within less than a year after he took office, Democratic leaders of the South forced it back into politics in the celebrated Kansas-Nebraska bill. The first bill reported to the Senate had no mention of it. If the com-promise of 1850 had settled the whole question, there was no reason to mention it. Yet a Kentucky Senator, backed by the whole South, forced the situation. Douglas, chairman of the Senate committee, was confronted with either throwing away the political position won by his entire career or going with his party in doing over again in more formal way what had already been done. If he did the first he would be powerless for good; if the other, he might influence his party's course later. Moreover, he thought—and so avowed in private, though he could not proclaim it in public—that the ultimate effect of the bill as pro-posed would be to promote freedom, that slave holding, in pushing this measure, was "helping to dig its own grave," to use his, own phrase.

James Buchanan has left it on record that when he went to Washington (to confer about the mission to England offered him), something more than two months after Pierce's inauguration, he discovered almost at once that the President and his Cabinet were shaping all their acts, appointments to office, and other acts, toward securing his (Pierce's) re-nomination and re-election. Buchanan himself had been an aspirant to the nomination for several years, and he probably knew the symptoms of the disease too well to be mistaken in the diagnosis. It was early to begin, too early in fact, for such untimely blossoming is often nipped by unexpected frosts. The President did, however, build up quite a Pierce party, going into the convention of 1856 with the votes of 122 delegates, while Buchanan had but 135. The Pierce party proved artificial by falling off at once, while the Buchanan vote gained slowly, and that for Douglas rose rapidly. He had grown more than ever conspicuous by the Kansas-Nebraska struggle, but, starting a hundred or more votes behind Buchanan, because of the pro forma voting for Pierce, the time and talk it took for him to gather momentum enabled Buchanan dele-gates to remind their colleagues of the dangerously swift growth of anti-slavery sentiment and the intimate way in which Douglas was identified with the immediate provocation of that growth, while Buchanan was not connected with it in any way, because he had only returned from Europe, where he had been for more than three years, a few days before the actual sitting of the convention.

Without doubt Buchanan was right in his diagnosis of Pierce's purpose, and he could not have been blind to the probability that he himself was being sent to England not at all as a distinction, but rather to shut him "out of the running" for the next term. The President was eager and urgent until he had pledged Buchanan beyond backing out, and then he grew cool, uninterested, slow about answering letters, and slower about getting definite instructions into Buchanan's hands, and hesitating, where he was eagerly positive at first, whether negotiations about questions between this country and England should be carried on by Buchanan in London or under his own eye in Washington.

If Buchanan did not suspect the motive before he went to England, it is reasonably sure that he did suspect soon after he arrived there, and he began at once to urge the appointment of his successor, and never slackened in that urgency, though no successor came until late in Pierce's term, too late for Buchanan, had he returned at once on the successor's arrival, to take any open part in promoting his own cause. He was left, too, during most of the time without a secretary of legation, and was obliged to perform all the drudgery of his office as well as the Minister's proper functions.

But those who schemed to put him "out of the running" did not justly estimate his indefatigable patience and industry, and when he returned on the eve of the convention, his canvass for the nomination was far more advanced than most of his opponents suspected, and because of that and the shock Douglas had given to the latent anti-slavery sentiment in his party in the North by his championship of the Kansas-Nebraska will, he (Buchanan) was enabled to secure the Democratic nomination in June, 1856.

Had Pierce been out of the way at first, and the struggle been squarely and openly between Doug-las and Buchanan, the chances are the nomination would have been given to Douglas, while he would have been at least as certain of election as Buchanan was as matters stood. In that event there would have been no great Senatorial campaign between Lincoln and Douglas in 1858, without which Lincoln could not have been nominated in 1860, and the course of history during the "sixties" must have been other than it was.

The Kansas-Nebraska excitement of 1854 and following had gone far toward solidifying anti-slavery sentiment and translating it into action, and in the campaign of 1856 it first appeared on a large scale in the country. But it was as yet largely an army of "volunteers," unaccustomed to acting together. The party had not yet come to "feel itself," so to speak, when its nomination was made. Fremont was in no sense a leader of men in politics, he had no "following" of his own, and the popular vote cast for him was purely the expression of an, as yet, crude and unorganized sentiment, as his nomination had been a kind of accident growing out of the excitement of 1854-- excitement of which it failed to take full advantage. His own father-in-law, Senator Benton, had bitterly opposed the Kansas-Nebraska bill, and still opposed it, but even he did not support nor even vote for his son-in-law. Not until the new party awoke, though defeated, to the fact that it had polled a million and a third votes, did it begin to appreciate its own strength and set some proper value on patient organization.

The increase in the whole popular vote for President between 1848 and 1852 was about 282,-000, yet, though Buchanan in 1856 polled about 237,000 votes more than were given to Pierce (something like as great an increase in the Democratic vote alone between 1852 and 1856 as there was in the whole vote of the country during the preceding four year term), yet the growth in the whole vote of the country, while the Democratic vote grew 237,000, was a little less than 900,000, of which total gain that of the Democrats was considerably less than one quarter. To the observant student of election figures it ought to have been plain that while the total gain revealed deepening interest in the political situation, as compared with the preceding four years, yet the relatively small Democratic gain revealed as clearly grave discontent in the ranks of that party.

The Whig organization had broken down and made no nomination, yet the nomination of Fill-more and Donelson by the American party, was very largely a desperate effort of confirmed Whigs to find some place where they could go. There was no reason in the so-called American-ism on which to found a national party any more than there had been in the "Native American!' movement which had broken down some years be-fore. Eliminating the word "native" from this name was part of the plan to open a way for Whigs who saw that their own organization had failed yet could not accept the old "Americanism," to join in the new. The vote for the new party was less than the whole gain in the popular vote, and was more than half a million less than the Whig vote of 1852. It should have been plain that many thousands of Democrats, not yet pre-pared to break with their party and enlist in an-other, were too nearly so to vote their own regular ticket. There could be, in existing conditions, but one cause for this, the yet but half awakened anti-slavery sentiment in both the old parties, which led many thousands of voters to refrain from voting altogether, a condition always likely to bring curious results, in this case to give Buchanan a plurality over Fremont of nearly half a million. It is one of many similar curious commentaries, too, on our way of electing Presidents that while Fremont, in 1856, with about 1,341,000 votes, secured 114 electoral votes, yet Douglas, four years later, with upward of 30,000 more votes, was given only 12, and Fillmore's vote gave him but 8.

The fantastic performances of the Whigs and their

candidate, Scott, in 1852, had killed that party, and the deep feeling, out of which grew the rising tide of anti-slavery sentiment, swept aside such little "remains" as it left behind it. In a large view Buchanan's triumph was one of mere organization, discipline, over an adverse yet un disciplined majority. Buchanan himself was not a leader of any magnetism, such as Clay, or even Douglas, or Blaine of a later day. Fremont was an unknown quantity, and Fillmore was too well known as weak, to say nothing of the narrow sentiment on which he stood. Buchanan was made President by the non-action of those who did not vote, rather than by the affirmative votes for him.

Despite all that was said in the North in ridicule of what was nicknamed "squatter sovereignty," it was growing clearer by 1856 that Doug-las was right when he declared privately in 1854 that under its operation there would never be another slave state, while the slaveholder could never avow that lie had not been given equal opportunity. And slaveholders saw this long before it was seen in the north. The one thing which more than any other had transformed the 166,000 free soilers* of 1852 into the million and a third of Re-publicans of 1856 was the drastic and arrogant Fugitive Slave law of 1850. The old law of Washington's time had merely commanded that fugitives "held to service in any state under the laws thereof" should not be withheld, when escaping into another state, from the pursuit of those

---

The Free Soil Party was a short-lived political party in the United States active in the 1848 and 1852 presidential elections, and in some state elections. A single-issue party, its main purpose was to oppose the expansion of slavery into the western territories, arguing that free men on free soil comprised a morally and economically superior system to slavery. It also sometimes worked to remove existing laws that discriminated against freed African Americans in states such as Ohio.

proving ownership in a prescribed manner. But it did not require the people living under different laws to take any active part in returning fugitives. The claiming owners must be their own slave catchers. The new law commanded all, no matter how much they abhorred slavery, to turn out at the bidding of the owners and help in remanding fugitives to bondage, and created Federal officers bound to transmit and enforce the bidding of the slave owners. At that odious requirement the gorge of practically the whole north rose, and not one in 20, perhaps not even one in 50, of the men who voted for Buchanan in the free states would willingly obey the requirement.

In 1852 this new law had hardly begun to bear fruit, but in 1854 came the fugitive slave Anthony Burns case in Boston, with some others not far from the same time, and by 1856 the harvest had increased and wrath grew hotter, though much of it not yet inflamed to action. This feeling it was that made the campaign of 1856 more earnest, though less noisy, than those of 1840, 1844 and 1848. That of 1852 had been quiet because people then dwelt in a "fools' paradise" of fancied "settlement." That of 1856 was too greatly ear-nest to deal much in noise and torch lights and tinkling songs. There was not a little passionate declamation, but it was largely confined to the enthusiasts of the anti-slavery sentiment busily blowing the new flame into vivid heat. The older and more disciplined forces of the Democratic party marched, for the most part, in rather sullen silence, but enough of them still marched to give Buchanan 174 electoral votes, and so bade him try his hand at keeping the peace, of which many of them had begun to despair.

CHAPTER X

The Opening Of The Storm

The Buchanan administration opened in an ominous calm, on the surface, at least, but really the southern politicians were amazed at the strength of the Fremont vote. They could not understand how Douglas and the other northern Democratic leaders had permitted so many voters to go astray, and the more or less vague distrust the south had felt, towards Douglas especially, was thenceforth strongly accentuated. The anti-slavery voters were themselves surprised. They knew their own strength for the first time, and did not yet know what to do with it.

The Dred Scott case, later to become so famous, had been in the Federal courts for two years or more, and final argument was heard upon it by the Supreme Court of the

United States in December, 1856, a month after Buchanan's election. Broadly stated, this was a suit by a slave against his master, claiming that lie was a free man by virtue of having been taken, by his master, out of the state of Missouri, where the master made his home and by whose laws the plaintiff had been held in slavery. In former cases the Missouri courts had ruled that taking a slave into free territory made him free, even when the owner took the slave only in a transient way and with no purpose of remaining. The State Supreme Court now overruled these decisions, and ruled that whatsoever effect taking the slave into Illinois might have in Illinois, when the bondman was brought back under Missouri law his former servile condition reattached at once. Then the slave was sold to a citizen of another state, and brought suit against him in the United States Circuit Court, which assumed jurisdiction and rendered a decision on a plea of the slave owner that the court had no jurisdiction, and from this decision an appeal was made to the United States Supreme Court.

It was determined not to make public the final ruling when made, lest it add to the excitement arising from the recent Presidential campaign and election. This was a foolish thing to do, in any view. It tended to magnify the importance of the case in the minds of the majority who knew nothing about it, and to disquiet even more those who knew the case, and knew that the court had only to decide, first, if the United States Circuit Court legally had the jurisdiction it exercised. If it were determined that it had no jurisdiction, that would end it, and every act of the Circuit Court in entertaining the suit would be as if it had never been, while if the lower court had the jurisdiction it claimed, then came the question, was its decision correct? To put it off for two or three months, as too inflammatory for present use, was to intensify the inflammation, and, to make the matter worse, it was widely asserted and believed that the Chief Justice had privately shown the decision to the incoming President, so that he might shape his inaugural and make other preparations accordingly.

It was a most unfortunate situation. All through the winter people guessed and wondered and the gossip makers "worked overtime." Much of the excitement would have subsided even then if, when the ruling was announced, it had appeared that the court had simply denied the jurisdiction of the inferior court for any reason and dropped the matter there. It did deny the juris-diction, but instead of stopping with that, went on to argue the whole slavery problem, assuming to declare that Congress had no power to make "needful rules and regulations" for the territories; that no power, except that of the state, or states, to be made out of the territory, could divest any slave owner who might take his slave into it, of his ownership in the slave and, of course, this could not be until the state should be organized and admitted into the Union.

All this could not have the force of law because all of it was outside the issues in the case adjudicated, but it pointed clearly enough to what would be declared the law whenever any case arose involving the points. It is impossible to convey to a man of today any adequate notion of the wrath of the anti-slavery men and the indignant disgust of the masses of the northern Democrats when this opinion—it was not, fairly, a decision—was made public in the spring of 1857. Only a reasonably firm conviction that the free state population would prove superior in capacity for peopling the new territory of the Union, and was already proving so in the territory of Kansas, was able to "keep the peace," and did so because it seemed clear that if superior in Kansas it must prove even more so in regions more remote from slave territory.

The whole of Buchanan's term of office may be fairly esteemed as part of—or indirectly preparing for it at least—the Presidential campaign of 1860. The meaning of the Dred Scott case, the turbulence and bloodshed in Kansas, the undisguised hostility of the slave holding people to Douglas because he clung to his own interpretation of the compromise of 1850, the whole current of events, tended to confirm the Fremont voters of 1856 in hostility to slavery, to determine other northern voters who had refrained from voting in 1856 to join in action with those who did vote and to push the supporters of the Douglas view a little further toward open anti-slavery.

The Democratic Convention met in Charleston, S. C., in April, 1860. Just as it was plain in 1844 that a majority of the convention was for Van Buren, so now it was plain that it was for Doug-las and his view of what should be party doctrine. The struggle was first over the platform. About half the committee reported on declaring, in brief, that neither Congress nor a Territorial Legislature could prohibit slavery in a territory, nor could even its people until duly admitted as a state, and that in the meantime it was the duty of the general government to protect slave property within the territory. The other half, save only the erratic General B. F. Butler, reported a plat-form reaffirming old Democratic principles in all other respects, and as to slavery agreeing to abide by the decisions of the Supreme Court. Butler alone reported the old platform of 1856. Butler's proposal was promptly and overwhelmingly rejected. Even the great mass of Democrats had gone beyond "glittering generalities" open to diverse constructions.

The Douglas platform was adopted by a considerable majority. That division of the party no doubt felt that to concede the promise to abide by Supreme Court decisions, including that in the Dred Scott case, was not to lose anything practical to freedom, because the free north had demonstrated both power and will to people and deter-mine the institutions of every new territory yet to be admitted. The southern wing of the party knew this fact quite as well, and knew that to yield was final defeat. With them slavery had become an obsession. Unless it could rule absolutely nothing else was of any worth. Therefore the seven coast states from South Carolina to Texas, with Arkansas and two delegates from Delaware, seceded formally and set up a convention of their own. After ineffectual balloting un-der the two-thirds rule the convention adjourned to meet in Baltimore in June.

Before it had there finished the preliminary business of filling the places of the Charleston seceders there came another secession, this time of the so-called "border states"— North Carolina, California and Delaware—and parts of four other states, together with the president of the convention, Caleb Cushing, of Massachusetts. The convention that was left nominated Douglas, and the seceders from Charleston and Baltimore, sitting separately, adopted the southern pro-slavery platform and nominated Breckinridge, of Kentucky (then Vice President under Buchanan), and Lane, of Oregon. The wreck of the old Democratic party was complete.

The story of Lincoln's nomination by the Re-publican Convention needs no retelling. No political event in our history is more familiarly known to all Americans. Lincoln himself had always been a Whig and the defeat of that party in 1852 had almost totally extinguished it in the north. But in the south it still had some life, and a few leaders who, unless it could be kept alive, would be like Othello—"their occupation gone." John Bell, of Tennessee, then ending a second term in the United States Senate, was one of these leaders and a man of ability and high character, but of the type which this generation calls a "back number." He still clung to the old idea of ignoring slavery, of permanently "removing it from politics," though it was plain to most of the world that that was impossible, because slavery had grown to be about all the "politics" there was.

They were too much awake to call the party they desired the Whig party, so they organized it with the name Constitutional Union party, smothering a little party with a cumbrous name, like a little boy in his grandfather's hat, and they nominated Bell, with Edward Everett, of Massachusetts. They had no sympathy with the dis-union element of the southern Democrats. As to slavery, they were more nearly in accord with the northern Democrats than any other active party; but old prejudice constrained them to "flock by themselves." They carried a few of the border states, and came near to carrying all of them, but they polled in the whole country only 589,581 votes. Had they given them to Douglas, with whose position they had more in common than with others, they would not have elected him, but they would have given him a popular plurality over Lincoln of 100,000 votes. They planted them-selves on the generalities of "the Constitution, the Union and the Enforcement of the Laws," shut-ting their eyes to the fact that nearly everybody professed devotion to the laws and to the Union, as they saw it, and that just what the Constitution meant was precisely what was—and about the only thing that was—at issue between the three greater parties.

With four parties in the field and slavery and freedom at last openly in a death grapple for the control of the national government, the whole people were stirred to the bottom. Except in the free states there was nothing such as might be called hand to hand fighting. South of Mason and Dixon's line, except for the relatively feeble activity of the Bell-Everett people in the border states, the southern Democracy, really the pro-slavery party, had it all their own way. In the free states their party polled, in round numbers, but 275,000 votes, and all but about 60,000 of these were cast in two states—Pennsylvania and California. South of that famous "line" the Douglas Democracy could make little mark and the Republican party none at all. North of the "line" the southern party, there known simply as "admin-istration Democrats," did only the little before remarked, and the Bell-Everett movement made scarcely a bit of ripple on the face of a boiling torrent.

But in the free states the Lincoln-Douglas conflict was waged hand to hand, and with a fervor and intensity unknown to this generation. Once at least, within the personal knowledge of the writer of these lines, Douglas, trying to reclaim an old personal friend from the ranks of the south-ern party, narrowly escaped being involved in a brawl that would have been politically fatal to him, among political friends and foes of whom every man present was armed. He extricated him-self only by his personal appeal to them and by risking his life in climbing along the outside of a rapidly moving railway train. In many cases the revolver of the speaker taking part in the heated public meetings, in the central west at least, was less likely to be forgotten than his armament of documents and statistics, and not infrequently was nearly as much in evidence to his auditors. There were great mass meetings and torch light processions, with ranks upon ranks of "Wide Awakes" and other uniformed marchers, but the great barbecues and feasts of earlier campaigns and other fripperies of campaign work were laid aside as out of place in the tremendous earnestness of the conflict, and political managers on both sides were more than chary of the old-fashioned "joint de-bates" as too dangerous in communities where the fires of political antagonism already burned so fiercely. It was enough to "get out your friends" and move them to vote. The men who saw that memorable conflict cannot forget it if they live a thousand years.

The depth to which the whole people were stirred was reflected in the popular vote which, while in the four years previous it had grown something less than 900,000 votes, swelled at a bound by nearly as much as before, though many did not vote at all. While the Buchanan vote, which elected him in 1856, had been in round numbers 1,838,000 in an aggregate vote of about 4,000,000, the Lincoln vote of 1860 was, again in round numbers, 1,866,000 in an aggregate of 4,676,000, or very far short of a majority. His plurality over Douglas was nearly half a million, but as compared with the whole Democratic vote for Douglas and for Breckinridge, he would have been nearly as much in a minority, conclusive proof of the bald political folly—ignoring the southern secession craze, and from the point of view of the Union—of the Democratic schism. Truly one is again reminded of the hackneyed but significant "Whom the gods would destroy," etc. The vote for Lincoln by the people, 1,866,352, was less by 944,149 than the combined vote of his opponents, and yet he had a majority of 57 of the electoral vote.

But little of this revolutionary result is to be ascribed, in a heroic sense, to Lincoln, either as a leader of men or as a man in himself. He had not been widely known. His conflict with Doug-las two years before had given him more fame than all the rest of his life. His own consummate shrewdness as a politician, added to and guiding that of his immediate friends, gave him the nomination. But the great army of voters who made him President were not followers of his more than of any other man of ability of like convictions. They were devotees of a certain political creed as the only means of preserving a national life and unity worthy of preservation. They were followers of a great and lofty faith, not of any man. It was that faith that made the revolution— not any leader. It is a great mistake, to which men are prone, to see the past too much in the light of the present. We must not read back into 1861 as the dominant incentive to men's action, what Lincoln had grown to be in their esteem in 1864.

In 1861 they would have followed Seward as faithfully, just as the Army of the Potomac obeyed Grant as loyally as it did McClellan. There must, indeed, be preachers and apostles of the faith, but the faith itself must be before and greater than they.

CHAPTER XI

Near To And After The End Of The Storm

Neither Lincoln nor any other thoughtful re-publican could sincerely claim that so tremendous a struggle in arms as the civil war could be fought out without mistakes of many kinds, or without more or less frequent wrong, injustice and needless suffering. They felt forced to de-fend publicly their acts, many of which they would admit to themselves were errors or even wrongs, because those acts were publicly at-tacked by the disgruntled of every shape and shade. There were divisions and discontents among themselves, but while the war lasted the great mass of the party which the war, and what led to it, had welded and held together, felt that it must remain true to itself as a party, even if many of its acts must be thought mistaken, until the great end of holding the nation together as a unit should be finally accomplished or finally defeated.

They felt, too, that their leader had, in the trial of a gigantic war, proved his substantial wisdom no less than his patriotic sincerity. Therefore when, in 1864, it was plain to intelligent observation that the end of the conflict was not far away, and that how it would end was little less assured, the party decided, justly, that the leader who had guided to that end was entitled to the fruit of his labors, and lie was placed in nomination for a second term.

The nearness and the well-nigh assured nature of the end of the conflict were just as much with-in the vision of the democratic party and its policy as an aggregation of wise and patriotic men should have been even more obvious. No matter how strongly it might disapprove the methods by which the war had been carried on, it was clear that its end was near, and as a hundred to one that that end would be success. But whether success or failure, democratic policy and duty pointed to the necessity of aligning the party primarily with an eye to the future. It was well enough, it was a duty perhaps, but not the most imperative duty, to put itself on record in condemnation of the methods of its political antagonist in the management of the war, but, unless it had given up, abandoned, its creed of principles upon which the federal government should be conducted, it should have addressed its most earnest thought to readjusting that creed to meet the necessities of the federal union, reunited in whole or in large part, as was then plainly inevitable after the terrific ordeal of civil war, and, having so determined the new application of its principles, to proclaim them frankly, boldly and clearly.

Instead of following this course, or any approach to it, it called its convention to meet in Chicago July 4, 1864, and then postponed it to August 29, and when it thus had two months more in which to reflect and to see more clearly the approach of the end, it proclaimed a platform of six resolutions, not one of which declared a shred of political principle of any kind, nor turned even a single glance toward the future. Except for a single expression of sympathy with the volunteer soldiery of the Union who had fought the war, every line of it, from beginning to ending, expressed nothing save bitter condemnation of all which they and their leaders had done, as practically criminal blunders, and crowned this vain pessimism about the unchangeable past with a declaration that the whole war was an unmixed failure, when, let the blundering have been what it might, the falsehood of the declaration was manifest to all the world but themselves. No matter how enormous and needless may have been its cost, even the purblind French emperor saw then that as to primary aim it was not a failure. And then the convention capped this crown by nominating the general who, whatsoever might have been his virtues and his merits as man and soldier, was the then most conspicuous representative of the "failure" it condemned.

No great political party ever made a more needless and senseless blunder. It was seen to be an egregious blunder by many thousands even at the time, and in the light of subsequent events it has become wholly incomprehensible how a party so capable of better things could be so recreant to its patriotic duty and so blind to its opportunities.

And yet, though it was all this, so potent was the stress of organization and so strong and vital the growth of the nation even in the midst of war, that, despite the fact that eleven States of the Union did not vote at all, despite the defection of many thousands of "war democrats" who voted for Buchanan in 1856 and for Doug-las in 1860, but now joined the republican ranks, and despite all the waste of war and the un-worthiness of the attitude taken by the convention, McClellan in 1864 polled within less than 30,000 of as many votes as were given to Buchanan in 1856, and only 400,000 fewer than both Douglas and Breckenridge in 1860, a number very curiously close to the Lincoln plurality over Douglas.

Despite all the waste of war and the aforesaid absence of eleven States from the roll call of 1864, the aggregate vote for both candidates was 4,024,792, or only about 650,000 less than the whole vote of 1860, and, again, it seems curious that this decrease in the whole vote was so near to the whole vote given to Breckenridge and Lane in 1860, less the number cast for them in the free States.

The campaign was, in the nature of things, narrowed to war considerations alone, since the party in opposition to the government refused to hold any principle or policy of its own. There was much acrimonious talk pro and con, but it was very largely such, on either side, as might arise in war time under any kind of government, and little if anything of the nature of free political discussion under a government guided by parties. It took a long time for most of the ultra democrats to see that John Quincy Adams, in the House of Representatives twenty-five years earlier, was wholly right when he warned the turbulent fire-eaters that the one only safety for slavery lay in their keeping the peace, because slavery can exist only by force of local statute law, and in war all laws are silent under the sword, and if they appealed to war their slaves "would not be worth five years' purchase." He gave more than twice too much time. They did appeal to the sword in April, 1861, and less than two years later the sword had shorn the shackles from every bondman.

It took a good many republicans, too, quite as long to learn that though war silences and suspends the laws of peace, yet it has laws of its own, just as truly grounded in human reason as are the laws of peace, by which it and its conduct must be governed, else it ceases to be war and degenerates into mere brawl and rioting.

The leader entrusted with a second term had but just entered upon it when the hand of an assassin thrust itself in and decreed that during nearly all that term the people should be guided and governed by another leader of whom few had ever thought as a leader. It is strange, too, that they gave so little thought to the kind of man chosen for the alternative office, since it was then but recent history that twice within a single decade the Whig party had elected a President and been practically politically betrayed by the two men who succeeded when the elected Presidents died, one of them but a month old in office and the other but little more than a year. Twice since 1864 the republican party has been robbed by death of the President it had chosen, but on both occasions the alternative advanced to the place proved to be worthy of the trust, and we may at least indulge the hope that this points to the exercise by the people of greater care in planning for the future of governing.

This time the loss was disastrous for both the party and

the country. There was doubtless fault on both sides in the schism between An-drew Johnson and Congress, each exasperating the other beyond otherwise probable action. Just here, however, the quarrel is pertinent because it gave rise to a situation which went very far toward pointing to the next President. Early in August, 1867, the quarrel brought about John-son's removal, or suspension, of Secretary of War Stanton, and his appointment of General Grant, already in command of all the army, to fill the place ad interim.

It has happened more frequently than many thinkers have been disposed to approve that a successful soldier has been elevated to the Presidency. It had happened with Washington, Jack-son, Harrison and Taylor before Grant's time, but it should not be overlooked, in considering such action, that of the four who preceded Grant in' that way Taylor alone had been a professional soldier and without experience in public service as civilians, so that the people knew something of them except Taylor otherwise than as soldiers. Looking at it from a later point of view, it should not be forgotten, either, that the only other at-tempts to make Presidents of successful professional soldiers wholly or nearly destitute of civil experience, in the cases of Generals Scott, McClellan and Hancock, all resulted in failure before the people, so that military fame alone has failed in that great tribunal in America oftener than it has succeeded. Neither had Grant been wholly without experience simply as a citizen, for he had been out of the army for quite a number of years prior to 1861, though he had never achieved much success as a man of business.

No doubt his great military fame was in 1868 the chief

factor in his supposed popular avail-ability, but it was known to all, and more especially and intimately to all the executive and legislative officials of the government whose judgment goes far toward guiding political public opinion, that in a time of great and bitter excitement, when he was already burdened with heavy duties as commanding general, Grant had had suddenly saddled upon him, besides his other duties, all the onerous civil duties of a cabinet officer as Secretary of War, and though lie knew that he was being used only as a stop gap in an emergency, had yet discharged them not only with irreproachable fidelity but with distinguished ability and with such a high sense of impartial probity as to leave behind him scarcely a trace of grievance even in that time of partisan acerbity unsurpassed in all our history, and, moreover, that when the Senate, under the tenure of office law, had refused to assent to the removal of Stanton, he had stepped aside with the quiet courtesy of the gentleman and the high respect for established law of the best type of the good citizen.

It is quite safe to say that knowledge of these facts, especially by those in the best position to know the truth, was no small factor in the readiness of the party leaders among the republicans to give him the nomination for President in 1868, nor was the knowledge that he had made practically no effort in his own behalf without very considerable influence in the same direction.

It was an indication of returning sanity in the democratic party that it named for its Presidential candidate Governor Seymour, of New York, one of the country's very ablest and most distinguished citizens, against whom, apart from the acerbities growing out of the civil war, there was no word of reproach. It was a slight further indication of returning good sense that one of the resolutions in its platform had something to say in favor of one of the old and honored doc-trines in the party policy, that of a tariff on imports for revenue for the payment of the costs of government. The declaration. was weakened by an added phrase about "incidental protection." It would have been better to have left that to be understood. That the revenue must be had no-body would deny to be imperative. If, in securing that, "protection" was extended over any-thing, it must, in democratic theory, be unavoidably incident. It had no place in any democratic definition of the purpose of a tariff. If it came along with the primary or only purpose of revenue, well and good. If it did not so come, then so much the better.

But with this glimmer of real democratic doc-trine the party sanity in the platform ended. The rest was unmixed condemnation of the party's opponents. It denounced negro suffrage, and therein, whether right or wrong as to present policy, it ignored accomplished facts as to citizenship, and antagonized its own old theories of suffrage, its only excuse being that the basis of citizenship had been changed. Worse than this, it expended most of its energy in denunciation of republican methods of "reconstruction" in the lately insurgent States. Whatsoever may have been the errors in the measures adopted, it was again in vain to do more in the party plat-form than express disapproval. It did this vehemently, and ended with that. It offered nothing of its own, good or bad. Worst of all, it forgot the party's long record in support of "honest money," and insisted on paying the holders of the nation's bonds in "greenbacks," because they were used in buying the bonds and had then been and still were at a discount.

In the methods of the campaign there was some further advance toward more rational management, though there was little real discussion of principles or policies. So far as these were considered at all, the discussion came from one side only. The other was merely opposition, apparently purely for the sake of opposing something. There were great meetings, marching organizations—survivals from those of war time—and torch lights and music and noisy cheering. But they were all, more obviously than ever, merely means for waking the phlegmatic to the fact that there was an election and "getting out" the voters. The fantastic features of the old times were less than ever in evidence.

Of the eleven States not voting in 1864 only three remained out, and the aggregate vote rose from 4,024,792 in 1864 to 5,724,684, an increase in four years of 1,700,000 votes. There were no "side shows" of vain little factions on trivial, make-believe issues. It was a "straight away race" between the dominant republican party and "the field," united for the time under one leader, and Grant's popular majority was 305,458, which, all things considered, was not a very large one. But, like _Mercutio's wound, " it served," and carried with it, as majorities do not always do with us, an electoral majority of 134. The opposition polled more than 471/2 per cent of the popular vote, but only a fraction more than 27 per cent of the electoral vote.

CHAPTER XII

Near To And After The End Of The Storm

Before Grant's first term in office expired, to some extent, perhaps, even before it begun, the solidarity of the republican party showed signs of approaching weakening. While the war for the Union continued the tremendous pressure from the outside exerted by that conflict held the party together as with bands of steel. The com-mon characteristic of all its members was the resolve to preserve and maintain the integrity of the nation. This resolve involved hostility to slavery because it was that "peculiar institution" which caused and was sustaining the as-sault on the nation. So long as slavery abstained from or concealed enmity toward the Union, the affirmative anti-slavery party in the free states — the party desirous of interfering with it where it existed by force of local law—was very small. The people of the north did not wish it for them-selves, but, though so far hostile to it, the immense majority of them did not feel that they had any right to take it away from those other political communities which did desire it. After winning Texas, the supporters of slavery began to grow aggressive and threaten to extend the institution into the national territory yet un-organized, in which the larger portion of the nation felt that it had the larger interest simply because it was the larger portion. And it was only then, when slavery was thus employed as an aggressive political force, that the party desiring to use hostility to it as a political force showed any indication of growing into dimensions that could justify uneasiness in even the community most zealously favoring it for its own uses.

Later it attacked the nation and threatened to dismember it, and the immediate effect was to consolidate into one party all who did not affirmatively approve slavery and did affirmatively desire to preserve the national entity. Before that time the people had been divided into parties based on differences of opinion purely political. In the new party, therefore, were found men of all varieties of earlier political opinion, the few survivors from old federalism, a large portion of the Whigs of later years, and very many of the Democrats who were the political descendants of the early strict constructionists. These latter had, indeed, preserved their organization, while those of the Federalists and the Whigs had been completely broken up, and many of them became "war Democrats," temporarily acting with the Republican defenders of the Union as a nation, while still other

Democrats preferred to adhere to their own organization, though freely voting, and fighting, with the Republican friends of the nation while danger to it threatened.

But now that the successful outcome of the defensive war had removed the pressure that had welded these heterogeneous elements into a unit of resistance against that danger, the same differences of opinion that had divided parties before the war began to reassert themselves. Men began to say, "I have never been a Republican party man except upon the issue forced on the country by slavery, and that is no longer a question." It was an entirely natural and legitimate thing. It was even a necessary thing to healthy national life. There were parties before slavery undertook to dominate all other interests. It was to be expected that like divisions would arise now that slavery was destroyed.

For this legitimate division there was a relatively free field in the free states, but in the south it was different. Slavery was destroyed, but the slaves remained, now freedmen, and dread of the danger of "negro domination," no matter whether real or only fancied—and the course of practical reconstruction seemed to justify thinking it real—operated in the former slave states to prevent the opening among the white people of the old lines of party cleavage, or of any new lines, and consolidated the whole white population into one party of resistance to the rule of the former slaves, or even their participation in governing. And so consolidated it remains to this day, and will remain for some period whereof no man can yet foresee the end.

In the free north there was no such danger, or fear of it. Both Whigs and Democrats there, as a rule, opposed slavery for their own uses before the war, but when the Whig party went to pieces after its defeat in 1852, it was natural that its members should gravitate largely into the new Republican organization, and when the war pressure was relaxed, the party leaders began to see that, slavery gone, the party must have some other affirmative reason for existence. The Whig ingredient in the party, larger at first, grew relatively more so as Democrats gradually dropped back into their continuing organization, and Whig tendencies, toward protection, toward internal improvement theories modified by changed material conditions, toward national control of banking, also modified from the old form, not to speak of others, became the controlling element in the party. The one-time Whig party had largely inherited the federalist tendencies toward centralization, or nationalization, it may be, per-haps, more justly called, and carrying them into the Republican party made it heir to them in its turn.

And so, while Grant was in his first term the "Liberal Republican" movement took shape. Some of its leaders, Greeley and Adams, for ex-ample, not of Democratic antecedents, grounded their action on more lenient views of reconstruction, but men like Chase, Trumbull and Palmer, Democrats in sentiment till silenced by the trumpets of slavery, made its more conspicuous leadership. By 1872 it had assumed such pro-portions, in the eyes of its leaders, that it held a national convention on May 1st in Cincinnati. The preponderance of the Democratic element was plain in the platform it proclaimed, more like that of the old party than any such structure launched within more than thirty years, almost wholly so, save for a most undignified "straddle" on protection. The old Whig element in it, how-ever, having so generously sacrificed itself on the platform, was placated by giving it the nomination in Greeley, a Whig from his youth.

By some magic which Democrats to this day wonder at, the regular Democratic convention in July accepted this nomination and platform by huge majorities. The platform was right enough, but Horace Greeley, as a nominee of their party, was enough to have evoked the ghosts of Jefferson and Jackson in fiery wrath. Grant was given the Republican nomination for a second term by prompt "acclamation," and the battle was on, in some respects the queerest in our history. Greeley had never been known save as a foe to the Democratic party. In 1841, when he was 30 years old, a printer as yet known to but few, he founded the New York Tribune, a rabid, uncompromising Whig paper, and for years even more ultra as an advocate of abolitionism. A man of great intellectual ability, he had made his paper and himself more virulently hated by pro-slavery men and dreaded by the Democratic party than almost any others of their antagonists. A man of intellectual eccentricity no less than ability, he had unsettled the confidence of many who agreed with him as to Whig doctrine and abolitionism, because he had given the use of his columns to the Socialists of that day, the Bloomerites, the "advanced thinkers' on the relations of the sexes, the vegetarians, the woman's rights freaks, and about every other "ism" that went straggling, a kind of intellectual hobo, across the mental vision of men and women. When secession was threatened in 1860-61, he had, in his great journal, gone so far into political freakism as to advocate letting the states involved go scot free,—carrying their slaves with them, of course —and even helping them to set up housekeeping, so to speak. A more grotesque candidate, for the Democratic party, could not have been found.

A portion of the party, and at first quite a large portion, disgusted and indignant, held a convention in Louisville of "straight-out Democrats," and nominated Charles O'Connor, a very distinguished New York lawyer, and John Quincy Adams, son of the former President of that name, and though these men positively refused the nominations, and thousands of those Democrats who had at first approved the Louisville movement were soon drawn back into the ranks of the "regulars" by the steady pressure of organization and habit, this dead Louisville ticket yet polled 30,000 votes in November. Among the Republicans, there were some surprised curses over the apostasy of one of the "old guard" of the anti-slavery forces, but for the most part there was vast laughter of the kind that political reporters call derisive, and in truth the campaign had in it not a little of broad comedy. Greeley had been always a bitter foe of the party that now, at the bidding of its subordinate officers, set him at its head as leader, and Gratz Brown, the candidate for Vice President, had been one of the original, ante-war Republicans, but it proved grim tragedy enough to the erratic, eccentric old man at the head of the ticket. The vote killed him. Before the month which witnessed his overwhelming defeat was ended, he lay in his coffin.

In strange contrast with the grotesquely pathetic leader of the Democracy and the wry faces at seeing it in his hands, of thousands who followed the standard he now bore, there was obviously a deepening interest in the questions dis-cussed before the people by the speakers of either party. Democratic orators were shut off from all glorification of their "standard bearer," but there was far more of the dignity and earnestness of genuine political debate in their treatment of the questions raised by the opposing plat-forms. They turned gladly from matter of personal panegyric, impossible save in a half-hearted way, to debating those questions,—save only as to the "straddle" on the tariff,—and the crowds of people who came out to hear, listened to discussions more really political than any that had been heard for twenty years, and listened with a plainly deeper interest. They tried hard to think and feel that party principle, and not the pro tempore party leader, was "the thing." In that respect the campaign had the tone of genuine politics again in very large degree.

But notwithstanding this plain reversion to-ward an older and healthier political condition than had been known for more than a quarter of a century, when it came to actual voting it was made equally clear that there was fatal lack of confidence that the men set up for high places by the party leaders were at all devoted to the prin2iples they nominally championed. Between 1864 and 1868 the aggregate popular vote was in-creased 1,700,000 votes, while between 1868 and 1872 the growth was only about 740,000. It was true that during the first of these periods eight states which had not voted in 1864 did vote in 1868, but so also three states not voting in 1868 were now added to the roll, now once more full, and the difference of five of the relatively smaller states restored to the list did not account satisfactorily for the falling off of nearly a million of votes in the aggregate increase.

It only needed to look to the vote cast by the two leading parties to find the explanation. While Grant was given nearly 600,000 more votes in 1872 than he received in 1868, the vote for Greeley in 1872 exceeded that for Seymour in 1868 by only 124,466. Making fair allowance for the growth arising solely from the voting for Greeley of three states more than voted for Seymour, it seems plain that had those three states remained out of the roll the Greeley vote would have been actually smaller than that for Seymour, especially since those three, Mississippi, Texas and Virginia, are among the larger of all the restored states. Grant, therefore, gained nearly 600,000 votes between his first election and his second, while the opposition vote practically made no gains at all, and he was elected by a plurality over Greeley alone of 762,991, and a majority over all of 727,975, or but little less than his plurality over his nearest opponent.

The conclusion seems unavoidable that between three-quarters of a million and a million Democratic voters wholly refused to vote for Greeley, and the conclusion is made the more positive when one finds the Tilden vote, four years later, nearly a million and a half larger than Greeley's. No more significant indication of the suicidal folly of any political party sacrificing fidelity to its honest party principles, when it has any, for the sake of mere "availability," aside from principle, is found in our political history.

CHAPTER XIII

The Most Critical Of Campaigns

Several reasons have been assigned for the marked growth in the Democratic vote after 1872 for some years. Popular impatience with the Republican party because it persisted long after the war was over, in brandishing the arguments and the passions of war time,—in continuing to "wave the bloody shirt," as it was called,—was one of the reasons. It was forgotten that a large number of Republicans had become such chiefly because of their detestation of the assault on the national life, and that most of these men found themselves reduced to choosing between this kind of argument and appeal and argument and appeal on behalf of doctrines which only a little while before had been distinctively Whig, and therefore they were wholly hostile to.

It has been often said that the discovery of corrupt abuses among government officers during Grant's second administration was a potent rea-son. It is not very complimentary to the intelligence of people to think thus of them. The larger the crowd the more scamps it is likely to contain. No man is a thief or a boodler, or any other variety of scamp, because he avows the principles and votes the ticket of one party or another. Judas was not a traitor because he was a disciple of the Master he betrayed. A goodly number of men are prone to feel at first that a church or a political party ought to be held responsible for the sins of its members, but they do not, as a rule, persist very long in any such absurd notion.

These and other similar circumstances no doubt had more or less weight, but a much more potent reason was the natural reaction from the depression of the war and the revival of interest in affirmative party doctrines. No political party can be long maintained on mere negation.

In accounting for the sudden swell in the Democratic vote in the partial elections of 1874 and also in the national election of 1876, scarcely enough emphasis has been laid on the effect of the financial convulsion of 1873 and the business depression that followed. For some queer reason our people have always acted as if they believed each of our marked monetary panics to be a kind of visitation of God on the political party happening to be in power at the time, and especially on its office bearers. The wide spread panic of 1837 destroyed Van Buren, who was President at the time, breaking down the party that had been really dominant since 1800.

The effect of the crash of 1857 happened to fall in with the shattering of the Democratic Marty and the springing up of the new Republican party which preceded the Civil war, and it is difficult to distinguish its political effect so clearly, but it may be taken as sure that the popular revulsion away from the Democratic party was very greatly forwarded by this wholly non-political cause, and the same kind of effect has been repeated on several later occasions. It was the more marked in its political effect in 1873 be-cause its first breaking out was in the collapse of the banking house of Jay Cooke & Co., which had been so conspicuously identified with various government financial transactions. There can be no doubt that this was one of the capital causes of the amazing change of more than a million votes which transformed the Republican majority of more than 700,000 votes in 1872 into a majority of nearly 350,000 against it in 1876.

It was a strange campaign in several respects. Tilden, nominated largely because of his participation in the relentless exposure and prosecution of the Tweed gang, a man of first rate ability and unblemished character, was by far the most formidable candidate the Democrats had named for many years, since even the acerbities of the war had largely passed by him, and the lapse of time was in his favor.

The Republican convention was in Cincinnati in midsummer, the same in which Ingersoll made his famous nominating speech, likening Blaine to a "plumed knight." That statesman was then beyond doubt the most eminent living Republican, as a representative of the party, and was as surely far in the lead of the half a dozen men talked of for the nomination of his party. It was a very hot summer and Washington is one of the hottest summer places known in this country. On the Sunday before the sitting of the convention, walking to church in the sweltering heat, Blaine suffered a serious sun-stroke, and when Ingersoll made his "plumed knight" speech it was hardly yet assured that the "knight" would recover his normal bodily condition. There were persistent rumors that he was dead flashing among the delegates more than once, and though, with nearly 300 votes on the first ballot, lie led very decidedly, yet many grew fearful that he could never live out the term, even if he would live to begin it, and his vote soon fell off, the nomination at last going to R. B. Hayes, who had just added to a good name as a soldier a most excellent reputation for integrity, ability and courage as Governor of Ohio. It probably seems a hard saying, but so far as humanity can see, if Blaine had not tried to go to church that hot Sunday morning he might have been made President, for his candidacy would have injected far more enthusiasm into the campaign than did that of Hayes, who was little known outside of Ohio. At all events that unfortunate sun-stroke quite certainly cost him the chance to try in that year. Eight years later, he faced other issues, and the war was eight years further in the past.

Down to the election, when presidential campaigns since 1824 had virtually ended, this was not a very enthusiastic one on either side, though marked by a still further advance of the Democratic party toward planting itself on affirmative grounds, but between then and the declaration of the electoral vote in February, 1877, it became the most peculiar, complex and critical in our his-tory. The Republican vote showed nearly half a million gain, but the whole vote had grown nearly two millions, and all but about one hundred thou-sand of the million and a half gain other than Republican, was cast for Tilden. The Democratic party had made about its normal gain as compared with the Republican, and the nearly a million voters who abstained from supporting Greeley four years before, had gone back to their old allegiance. Tilden's plurality over Hayes was 250,935, and his majority over all was 157,037.

It was very far from the first time that a candidate with as popular majority had been defeated in the electoral college, but this time it was by a margin of only one vote, as claimed by the Republicans, while the disorders in three of the southern states, with some foolish blundering in Oregon, seemed to throw doubt on the vote of those four states which, if sustained, would turn the scale the other way. There was tremendous popular excitement and much wild talk of pre-venting the inauguration of either by force, if in no other way. Congress shared in the passions of the hour, but they were held in check partly by the firm attitude of the Grant administration, and quite as much by the patriotic good sense of Tilden and the mass of the Democratic voters, all of whom submitted, not without a vast deal of heated argument and loud grumbling, but without any violent resistance, to the creation by Congress of the purely extra-constitutional device of an electoral commission of 15, which, by the long famous 8 to 7 vote, gave all the disputed points in favor of Hayes, who was peacefully inaugurated and served out his full term with unquestioned credit to himself and honor to the nation, though not altogether to the satisfaction of his party.

The history of that threatening crisis is probably more familiar to most Americans than any other political event now so far in the past, and need not be detailed. It is probably generally ad-mitted now that the commission administered the strict law of the case, as it was in honor bound to do, as nearly as was possible. But it is not out of the way to say that on a fair construction of the constitution as related to Presidential elections, Congress had no more right to create that commission than to enact laws for any foreign country.

The framers of the constitution hesitated long over the methods of electing the President, giving the power to elect first to Congress, then took it away and provided for electors, then dropped that provision and restored the power to Congress, and again took it away from Congress finally and created the electoral college as we know it, substantially. It gave to the state legislatures the plenary right and power to elect, or have elected, the electors of the President, in any manner which those legislatures, each for itself, might wish. It then provided that the electoral vote of each state should be sent to the President of the Senate, and by him be opened and counted and the result declared, iii the presence of the whole Congress sitting together in one room, but as separate organized bodies; and it further pro-vided that Congress might direct, but only by a general law to govern all cases, how the returns of the electoral votes of the several states should be authenticated to the President of the Senate.

Congress never enacted any such general law to govern the authentication of the electoral re-turns, and it was precisely on questions of such authentication that every disputed point in the election of 1876 arose. It was not the purpose of the Constitution that Congress should have any-thing to do with electing Presidents, otherwise than by sitting as witnesses of the counting of electoral votes by the President of the Senate, save only to provide that in a certain specified event the House of Representatives, voting by states, should choose between candidates where no candidate had a majority, as, for example, where the electoral choice was balanced by tie vote, and that power was for one house, and not for Congress as a whole, the Senate being con-fined to choosing, in such specified case, its own presiding officer only. It never contemplated that Congress should have any canvassing power, that is, power to decide what was a vote, or to make any objection to any electoral vote being received and counted or not counted. It, Congress, was commanded merely to sit as witnesses, the power and the responsibility of canvassing and receiving or rejecting all electoral votes, being concentrated in the President of the Senate, who, if he misused the power entrusted to him, might be adequately punished, while obviously Congress can never be punished.

Congress neglected to perform the duty specified for it in the enactment of a general law of authentication by which the several states and the President of the Senate should be governed, for violations of which the guilty state could be punished by losing its vote, or the President of the Senate be punished for misuse of his power, and then began, in 1801, little by little, to assume the powers of a canvasser or returning board, and continued to enlarge its own powers in that way down to the most conspicuous of its usurpations in 1876.

CHAPTER XIV

The Campaign Tide Turns

In 1872 the Democratic party had returned to sanity as a party so far as related to a platform of principles by which it proposed to stand, but, lured from discretion by the liberal Republicans, it forgot the sanity it had shown four years earlier in the selection of a candidate, and accepted Greeley, with the effect of keeping something like a million of its voters away from the polls on election day. By 1876 it seemed to have opened its eyes to the truth that both a frank declaration of principles and a consistent and worthy candidate are necessary to the continuous life of a political party in a free people. It accordingly framed a platform affirmative in character and in harmony with the historic development of the party, and placed on it a man of character and ability.

The result was that the disgruntled deserters of four years before returned to the ranks, the Marty made its usual gain from new voters, and the candidate led his chief opponent by more than a quarter of a million votes, and led all opponents combined by nearly 160,000. It would have been well for the party if it could have sustained the pace it had thus set for itself. One could frankly sympathize with its bitter disappointment that although so greatly in the majority before the people as a whole, the division of the country into states and the intervention of the electoral sys-tem deprived it of its popular advantage in the final result. It was not in any wise the fault of the party. It was only that more of the party's voters than were locally needed lived in some of the states, while not enough for success lived in others. If it could have redistributed its population as it might choose among the states, it would have been easy to wholly change the result. The solid and significant fact was that once more there was a good working Democratic majority of the people. It was pitiable weakness for Democrats to say, "What's the use," because well doing in both particulars united, had failed to win. The way to assure success sooner or later was to keep that working majority, and it should have been clear enough that the way to keep that majority was to persist in the well doing that made it a majority.

But when the party delegates assembled in convention they made a fairly representative declaration of principles, but they yielded,—as the old Whig party had done in 1840-48 and 52, as their own predecessors in the party had done in 1864, and as the Republicans had partly done in 1868 and 1872,—to the dazzle of military glory, and gave the nomination to General Hancock, who had been a professional soldier all his life, and never anything else.

Meantime there had been no abatement of the Whig coloring that had been imparted to the Republican party, more especially in electing to stand by the theory of protection. The mental character and tendencies in thought which made men Whigs in the middle years of the century, now, in the century's last quarter as inevitably made them Republicans. The responsibilities of control so long resting on that party had developed in its ranks an unusual number of able men and had, at the same time, fostered their ambitions. There was hardly room in any one political party for two such leaders as Conkling and Blaine, and there were others only less demonstrative than they had grown to be. Blaine felt that bad luck alone had cheated him of the nomination in 1876, and again he offered in 1880, while Conkling, for some reasons perhaps not yet clearly understood, resolutely pressed Grant for a third nomination, and Grant had, reluctantly as there was and is reason to think, yielded his assent to the movement.

The conditions made the Republican convention in Chicago in 1880 a memorable one for the excitement and stubbornness of the competition, and into this, Garfield, then just elected to the Senate from his state, but not yet having taken the seat, was thrown by being sent as a delegate from his state. He was bound to press the claims of Sherman, who was only less conspicuous as an aspirant than Grant and Blaine. Doubtless he thought he saw, in the strenuous rivalry between

Grant and Blaine, a chance to promote party harmony by a union on Sherman, but in working to-ward that end he made himself, whether consciously or not, so conspicuous and commanding a figure that lie suddenly found the whole matter taken out of his hands by an abrupt coalescence of nearly all the elements of opposition, not so much to Grant himself as to a third term for any man, and himself lifted to the place the others were struggling for. There were more than hints that the movement was not so spontaneous as it seemed, but no conscious self-seeking was ever brought home to him, though the bitternesses of the conflict were the seed, in large measure, of the feuds which a little later rent the Republican party, and in which Conkling was conspicuous. After the excitement of the convention, the campaign was for a long time a confused one, and its elements did not clarify till the Republican leaders discovered, rather late, from some queer tariff comment of Hancock and the puzzled treatment of it by his supporters, that the Democrats had so long been strangers to pushing any affirmative political principles at all, that they were quite unready to discuss the tariff, and from that moment Republican campaigners, familiar with the old Whig theories and arguments, pressed the warfare vigorously on that point more than any other, dropping the merely spectacular and making the campaign, from thence to the end, the thoroughly business-like proceeding for which their discipline fitted them.

Garfield secured a majority of 59 of the electors, but again the popular vote gave evidence, as on previous occasions, of the errors of managing leaders on the Democratic side and the discords among the leaders of their opponents. The whole vote exceeded that of four years before by less than 800,000 though in the former four years it had grown by two millions. Of the increase, a little more than 400,000 or about half, went to Garfield, while of the other half more than 300,- 000 was wasted on the "Greenback" and other side issues, and Hancock's vote exceeded Tilden's by only a little more than 60,000. Military glory, when not supplementary to any deeper interest or some vital principle, again failed to "make good." Garfield, though more than 300,000 in a minority of the whole vote, yet had a plurality of a few thousand votes over Hancock alone.

When but four months in office Garfield was struck down by the hand of a foolish assassin, and was succeeded by Chester A. Arthur, the Vice President, the one case in the four, including it-. self, which had then occurred in our history, in which the succeeding officer stood manfully by the party which had trusted him, proved himself a better and stronger man than even his friends would have claimed for him, and discharged his great trust with general satisfaction to the whole people. In a general way he had won a fair claim to be entrusted for a term of his own, but he encountered the obstacle sure to be met in any great and long successful party in our country. There were too many other strong men with older claims for party service who aspired to the trust.

Blaine, cheated by "hard luck" in 1876, and in 1880 swept aside in the stormy resistance to the third term movement, now came forward again. It must, by the way, have been interesting and exasperating for Conkling, when he antagonized the administration of Garfield early in 1881, to have to reflect that it was his own strenuous at-tempt to nominate Grant,—as much at least "to beat Blaine" as for any other purpose,—that made Garfield, now as much in his way as Blaine would have been, President. The soreness from the conflict of 1880 was by no means healed, but it affected Arthur, who was Blaine's chief competitor, nearly or quite as much as it did Blaine, and the older party man had relatively little trouble in outstripping his younger rival. It took but four ballots, on the same floor where the long and hot conflict of four years before had been fought out, to give him the nomination, and he entered on the campaign with strong confidence.

But conditions had changed. The Civil war had receded twenty years into the past. Reconstruction had been completed seven years before under President Hayes, and though that had been done in a way to go very far in his party toward relegating him to private life, yet it was an accomplished fact, and little could be done with it toward "warming up" more or less reluctant voters. The stirring war cries of the heroic age were obsolete. For twelve years the old Democratic party had been sloughing off the men identified with it when it was "on the wrong side," in a way, and had been steadily growing toward a new lease of life as a real political party with an affirmative policy. Eight years before it had actually won a large popular majority, though losing the fruit of it by force of a peculiar constitutional provision, and four years before, though it had foolishly lapsed into the weakness of "worshipping strange gods" and bowing down to the fancied glamor of the warrior's "brass buttons and gold lace," it had only narrowly missed another popular majority, really beaten mainly, perhaps only, by a monetary vagary, on another form of which it was to go to disastrous wreck in the near future. The whole people, practically, had grown far toward demanding of par-ties and their candidates less rhetoric and more affirmative action. We hear much of the de-cadence of our politics, but there is far less of it than flamboyant orators would have us believe. We need only to look back to the noise and dust and "whirlwind" success of 1840 to feel sure on that point. Methods have changed, but essential politics now is but little different—and that little is mainly improvement—from politics fifty or more years ago.

In the same year that saw the murder of Gar-field, a sturdy Democratic lawyer emerged from obscurity into some local fame by being elected mayor of the Republican New York city of Buffalo, and speedily won distinction by administering its affairs on plain, straight-forward business lines, and won also the soubriquet of "the veto mayor" by frequently extinguishing time-serving measures adopted by the city council which he thought violative of or indifferent to business principles, or conscientious administration.

In the next year, solely on his record as mayor. of Buffalo, he was given the nomination of his party for Governor of the state of New York, against the then national secretary of the treasury, who was believed to have been given the Re-publican nomination by direction of the national administration. He was an honest and capable-man, but the people of the state felt that it was only Democratic that they should be permitted "to manage their own domestic affairs in their own way," and therefore resented any "administration intervention."

Now, too, the Conkling-Blaine-Garfield-Arthur feuds in the Republican party began to bear fruit. immediately

116

affecting New York politics only, so far as men could yet see, but keenly observed by men interested in politics throughout the nation. Large numbers of men accustomed to call for and advise about Republican party action, now pre-served ominous silence. It was objected to the Buffalo mayor that he had had no experience in state politics and was equally without legislative experience of any kind, while even his executive experience had been brief and on a small scale. It was answered that it was not a legislator, but a governor that was in question, and that the Buffalo man's executive experience and action had all been precisely of the kind whereof the Etate stood in need.

When the votes were counted it was learned—by the nation as well as by the state—that the Buffalo man had beaten the administration Re-publican candidate by nearly 200,000 plurality, and beaten all contestants by more than 150,000 majority, a result then unprecedented. From the hour when that result was known, and was soon followed by public knowledge that the new Governor was administering the affairs of the state on precisely the same lines, mutatis mutandis, which he had followed in Buffalo, Grover Cleveland sprang at once into a factor in national politics which no political party could afford to over-look.

When the Democratic national convention met, in July, 1884, its platform reaffirmed distinctive principles of the party by which it had stood through many years, save only when driven from its moorings by the storms of war and its immediate consequences. One ballot was enough to determine the nomination, more than the required two-thirds vote being given at once to Cleveland.

The campaign was fought out, as a whole, by argument, generally temperate and earnest, on the several declarations of principles of the two parties. General B. F. Butler, of Massachusetts, who was sent to the Democratic convention from that state, after giving the convention fair notice that he would "bolt" from the nomination on the tariff plank of the platform, stood as a candidate on a greenback-labor kind of fusion plank, hoping to draw enough Democratic votes in New York to defeat Cleveland in his own state, and having secured the aid of John Kelly, then powerful as a Tammany leader in the city, Butler al-ways insisted that enough votes were cast for him to assure Cleveland's loss of the state, but that enough of them were fraudulently counted for Cleveland instead of for him, so that the state was given to Cleveland by some 1,100 plurality over Harrison. He declared that but for the ill-ness of Kelly he, Butler, would have been able to prove positively that state of things, but that without Kelly he could not institute the proceedings he intended, and the whole matter, there-fore, passed beyond recall. There is probably some truth in these and other charges of fraud,--always loud when an election is close, but it is just as probable that proven frauds would "cut both ways."

Cleveland himself took no active part in the campaign, and the only sensational incident was furnished by the blundering folly of one Rev. Dr. Burchard, who made a speech of welcome to Blaine at a kind of reception given to him in New York city only a day or two before the election. In this speech the reverend gentleman played, in truth, a role not unlike that of "the bull in a china shop," by characterizing the Democratic party as "the party of Rum, Romanism and

Rebellion," sacrificing the cause he professed to be trying to promote to a bit of "smart," impertinent alliteration. So far as Blaine was him-self was concerned, the whole affair was impromptu and unaffected, and it is said for him that he was so preoccupied during Burchard's speech, in thinking what he should himself say, that he did not hear the phrase, enough, at least, to "sense" it or to remember it.

Winning the state of New York gave Cleve-land an electoral majority of 37 votes, but in the popular vote there were again some queer results of our way of electing Presidents. The increase in the whole vote was nearly 850,000, and this gain was divided between the two leaders with a surprising approach to equality, Cleveland's vote exceeding Hancock's by 433,000, and Blaine's exceeding Garfield's by 403,000. Cleveland's plurality over Blaine was but 23,000, and yet more than 300,000 votes were utterly thrown away on St. John, Prohibitionist, and Butler, the Green-back-labor candidate. Probably most of the St. John voters would have voted for Blaine had St. John been out of the way, and in no other respect was his candidacy of any consequence whatever, while Butler's 173,000 votes were equally lost. If lie really desired the defeat of Cleveland on his tariff views, as he claimed, he should have frankly worked for Blaine. As it was, if his voters had any effect it went to strengthen, not weaken, Cleveland. And, once more, the successful candidate, while receiving 23,000 votes more than his nearest competitor—a small plurality, indeed, in a vote of more than ten millions—was yet in a minority, on the whole vote of more than 300,000.

CHAPTER XV

A new challenger in party lists

In 1885 Cleveland entered upon the discharge of his duties as chief magistrate of the nation, or nearly thirty years after Buchanan, the last Democratic President the nation had known, had assumed the same burden. When that last one of the old-line Democratic Presidents went out of office, the powder that was to open the great Civil war already lay awaiting its hour in the guns that frowned around Fort Sumter. The whole vote for and against that President was only a little more than four and a half millions. His first party successor went in under an aggregate vote of more than ten millions, yet the last one of the old order had nearly half a million plurality though over 350,000 in a minority of all, while the new one also won office in despite of a majority of more than 300,000 against him. In lasting political principles the creed professed by each was substantially the same. The "questions of the hour" which confronted each in his turn were widely different. Cleveland encountered at once a vast army hungry for office from a quarter of a century of fasting. They should not have been surprised at what was meted out to them, for the theory that "public office is a public trust" had been substantially that upon which he had acted in the offices he had held, that which had given him the public vogue that led them to make him their leader, and that which he had frankly declared should guide his actions if elected. He sent thou-sands of them home as hungry as when they came. He gave repeated evidence that he meant always to "do his own thinking," and to square his action with that thinking whenever it was humanly possible. He resisted stoutly, and in the main successfully, the same kind of Senatorial encroachment on the executive discretion out of which had grown some of the most dangerous feuds in the Republican party. He rebuked the squatters on public lands just vacated in the Indian Territory, and drove _them off as sternly as he rebuked Senatorial squatters on the domain of executive power to appoint and remove officers. He went to the length of using military power to protect Asiatic immigrants against the violence of lawless mobs, and he earned a claim to be called "the veto President," as well as "the veto Mayor," by refusing his assent to a hundred and fifteen of the less than a thousand bills passed in the first session of Congress after he took office, because he regarded them as primarily predatory on the public treasury.

It was inevitable that a course such as indicated by these

examples of what he did in his term of office, should breed many antagonisms within his party, notwithstanding the undesirable fact that his supporters had been given fair warning by him of what lie was likely to do as President.

Yet when the time came, in 1888, to nominate a candidate for the succession, though lie did not receive quite the spontaneous call given him four years before, he was called again to take the lead, and this time was opposed by the Republican, Benjamin Harrison, whose grandfather had won the Presidency nearly fifty years before in the great "whirlwind" ad captandum campaign of 1840. This Harrison had won a fine reputation as a. soldier of the Civil war, as his grandfather had done in the second war with England, and for all civic duties was confessedly a far abler and a far more cultivated man than his father John Scott Harrison, who had been a member of Congress before the Civil war, or his more famous soldier grandfather. So far as concerned public questions and the attitude assumed toward them by the two great parties, their declarations of principles and of policy, there was little difference now from the conditions of 1884. On the surface the campaign was conducted with comparative temperance and dignity. The fantastic phenomena of older campaigns had been almost entirely eliminated, and public discussions before the people were now addressed more directly to the reasons why one set of principles, or one policy of administration, should be preferred before another. Under the surface, however, there is reason to believe that there were currents of influence utilized of which the. general public saw little or nothing. It is not meant that this "still hunt" kind of work was not entirely legitimate. Doubtless much of it was so. It is only meant that it was directed in channels not before so effectively used. The difference, and its effect, will be indicated further on.

The popular vote showed some facts that were remarkable and significant in more than one way. While its growth in the two immediately preceding quadrennial periods had been, in each, not far from 800,000, it now rose suddenly to more than 1,340,000. It was a period of rapid growth in the whole population, but so much of this general growth was in non-voting immigrants, that this could not account for much of the swift voting increase. It indicated far more, a deeper and more wide spread interest in political questions and more searching and effective methods of get-ting out the vote. Only in the periods of the vital stir of the Civil war, again when the seceding states were being restored to the roll, and again in the Tilden revival of the Democratic party after the demoralization of the Greeley campaign, had this rate of growth been approached. Plainly some new feeling or method was entering into politics.

Of this growth, Cleveland's vote in 1888 exceeded that given him in 1884 by more than 660,-000, and Harrison's exceeded that given to Blaine in 1884 by about 590,000. There were three or four minor tickets, Prohibition, Union Labor, and some others, all of them together showing 411,967 votes, or about 90,000 gain over the "outside" vote of 1884. This was approximately a fair di-vision of the increase among the three classes of voters, the Cleveland excess probably representing largely that independent element among voters naturally leaning toward independence in ad-ministration. On this popular showing Cleve-land had a plurality of more than 96,000 over Harrison, but on the aggregate vote was in a minority of 315,309, while Harrison, behind Cleve-land near 100,000 votes, was on the whole vote in a minority of 508,625, and yet was the winner of the race.

Here conies in the under-the-surface part of the campaign, before adverted to. It was a foregone conclusion that the south would be "solid" for Cleveland. Therefore no use for anybody to waste any effort there. The lesson, not taught as a new thing, but deeply emphasized, by Cleve-land's winning in 1884 by a plurality of only 1,100 votes in one state, New York, was not lost, more especially on the thousands who probably felt like revenging their disappointment with the administration, but rarely to the extent of openly sundering their party ties. Nor was it any more lost on the politicians who make a business of conducting elections to win, and who, therefore, directed all their astuteness and bent all their energies toward the doubtful states, the places where the "getting out" of a few more hun-dreds in the popular vote might make a marked difference in the electoral vote. Other influences were doubtless of weight, but these were potent in making it possible for a candidate to have more than half a million majority against him among the voting population, and yet secure 65 electoral majority.

The period of the Harrison administration was relatively quiet, so far as regards opportunity for men in power to make much impression on the popular imagination, or in any way turn the current of some popular passion in their own favor. Nor was Harrison a man calculated to take advantage of such opportunity as might arise, to say nothing of creating it out of circumstances not spontaneously promoting it.

Those who may have, more or less furtively, contributed to Harrison's success in 1888 by way of resenting, or "getting even" for 1884 and the chill of disappointment that followed, now found themselves not a whit profited by it in any way. Moreover, the tightening of business conditions and stringency and vague menace in monetary affairs were felt, though few recognized what or why the uneasiness and discomfort were, in the last year of the Harrison term, while the campaign for his successor was in progress.

Harrison was named by his party for a second term, and though the prevalent uneasiness seemed to infect the Democratic party and threaten it with dissension, the cloud blew away, and for the third time in succession the Democratic national convention nominated Cleveland, the race, as to principals, thus being between the same two leaders as in 1888. Neither was a man to appeal much to the enthusiasm of mere crowds of people, and the events of both administrations by them, as well as the more or less dimly threatening business conditions of the election year, combined to turn men's attention mainly to economic problems and interests.

So far as party differences were concerned the tariff problem had risen above all other present questions. Cleveland had laid strong emphasis on its primal importance, and the consequent menace against the protective policy had provoked increased Republican devotion to it. Democratic opposition had heated to the point of antagonizing protection, not merely as an erroneous and unprofitable measure of policy, but as a positive wrong, which the national government had no right or power under the Constitution to impose on the people and their business, a kind of unconstitutional tax imposed on all for the benefit of a small favored class.

Before the people and in its public aspects, the campaign was contested mainly on this question, but it was plain to all who were active in the contest, and especially to those who "got close to the masses" while seeking to carry on the quiet, "still hunt" methods so effective in the preceding campaign, it was plain to all these that there was something stirring in the common mind which retarded their efforts. They could not define what it was. It seemed intangible and elusive, but something there was that created a vague and absent-minded kind of aloofness in the public feeling. Men could not be roused to take animated interest in the things in which the political workers wished them to take interest. To the veteran politician they often seemed to be foolishly drawn toward matters that to him were mere "side, shows" and of no consequence to "practical men," mere "rainbow chasing," in fact. The politician, intent on his own aims, felt this intangible something, but came to really "sense" it only after the campaign was over and the results known.

And when the results were known, some of them were surprising, indeed, as manifested in the popular vote. There was, as usual, a gain in the aggregate vote, but instead of approaching the nearly a million and a half gained in the preceding four years, it had fallen to only 668,-746. This was surprising in itself, but when the details were looked into the surprise was start-ling. Cleveland, in a vote, each time, of more than five and a half millions, had gained over 1888 only 14,582, as against his near 700,000 gain in that year over 1884, while Harrison, instead of making any gain over his own vote of 1888, had actually fallen below that vote by 254,971, thus giving to Cleveland, even with his own trifling gain, a plurality of 366,211.

Looking further, the surprise grew. Bidwell, the candidate of the Prohibitionists, had gained about 20,000 over the vote of his cold water party in 1888, a greatly larger gain, proportion-ally, than Cleveland's, but quite insignificant in the general result. Wing, a Socialist candidate, had polled 22,613 votes, practically "captured" from somebody, but still insignificant. But Weaver, the candidate of the new Populist party, —heir of the futile Green-back faction, and in part of the spasmodic "Labor vote," so-called, but far more than anything else the representative of the before-mentioned new and strange unrest in the drift of political thought and feeling,—had captured at a blow 1,035,128 votes, carrying with them 22 votes in the electoral college.

Practically the whole of this vote was a gain for a new party struck out in a breath, so to speak, and swallowing up at once Harrison's actual falling off of more than 250,000 from his former vote, and cutting off at the same time all of the gains which both the two great parties might have been expected to show in normal circumstances. Here was, indeed, a new and portentous phenomenon for the professors of practical politics, and one at which many of them stared in blank dismay.

It was, indeed, destined to work startling changes in some of the yet future campaigns for both the old parties, and it was well for, perhaps, both, and certainly for one, of them, that it thus challenged their attention four years in advance of the next election. Meantime, despite the Populist capture of 22 electoral votes, Harrison's disastrous loss of support gave Cleveland a larger electoral majority than in 1884, and. again the country was given a President in a large popular minority.

CHAPTER XVI

The Campaign Of Education

The second Cleveland administration began amid the mutterings of another financial storm, one that only a few of the exceptionally weather-wise had made any preparation for, or even suspected the extent of, though many had felt vague premonition of approaching trouble of some kind. It is a curious fact that nearly all of the more serious monetary storms we have encountered have fallen in the first year of some new national administration. That of 1837, probably the most disastrous relatively of them all, broke over Van Buren's head almost immediately after he had taken office. That of 1857 broke out with great fury in the middle of the first summer in Buchanan's administration, and for a time drew all men's attention away from the dread of an apparently impending war, wherein the skirmishers had already opened fire in Kansas. That of 1873 confronted Grant rudely in the summer of the first year of his second term. True, he had already been President for the whole of one term, but he had only just passed through the ordeal of an election, resulting in his complete overthrow of Greeley by the then unprecedented popular majority of nearly three-quarters of a million. Material changes had been made in the constitution of the cabinet, and changes in Congress indicated a firmer grasp of power by the Republican party. It was a new administration beyond doubt, though the chief administrant was a "hold over" from the past term. The convulsion of 1893 fell on Cleveland almost at the out-set of his second term, and was an especially "unkind cut" for him, since it grew largely from conditions against which he had offered stout resistance.

There were financial flurries and distresses be-fore 1837, and there have been others than those named since that date, but they have been minor in their consequences, as well as their immediate effect, and left a very much lighter impression in the public memory. The four mentioned, however, stand out boldly in the written history of the country, in the recollection of men and in tradition. There are many who can today talk glibly and intelligently of the extent and the effects of the panic of 1837, though they were not born till long after it was over, and many of them could not tell you the year in which the Constitution of the United States was adopted. The other troubles have been limited in range. These four swept over the whole people, and every one of them followed a Presidential election, well within the first year of a new national administration.

The only one of our really general financial storms which seems an exception to this apparent rule is that of the later year, 1907, but that trouble was preceded by a variety of very exceptional facts and conditions which probably hastened it. According to precedent in the meteorology of the business world, it was "not due" until 1909, and was pushed forward by some especially inflammatory causes. Moreover, we are not at all sure as yet that it may not be followed by a serious relapse in 1909, a result of "the patient getting up too soon," just as the paroxysm of 1837 was followed by another in 1839. It would be interesting to trace out the connecting lines, if any such there be, between financial storms and governmental periods.

Those of 1837 and 1857 were followed, also, by wide changes in political control at the next succeeding governmental periods. That of 1873 was not, nominally, so followed, since the Hayes administration succeeded Grant's second, but it stood for a very much softened type of Republicanism, and looked at from the popular point of view, it ought to have been a complete change, in name and otherwise, since the Democratic vote of the year before had been nearly 160,000 larger than those of all other parties combined. It is a strange proclivity in the people to thus seem to punish a political administration for a panic that breaks through the surface within its term, though it was quite certainly festering under the surface for years before that particular administration began. It seems a chronic habit, how-ever, though quite as absurd, on the whole, as to credit an administration for the good crops that ripen in its time.

It is highly probable that the financial disaster of 1893 would have proved fatal, for a time, at least, to Democratic supremacy in the government even without the strange mania for the coinage of silver, developed in the party at a time when most of the rest of the world had resolutely turned against it. But that extraordinary passion for a vain thing, as the world stood, settled its fate beyond a peradventure, at least until the rest of the world may be persuaded to go along with it.

Without going at all into the outworn discussion of what material mankind should use for its money, it is enough to say that there is no question of inherent right or wrong involved. Money is an instrument or tool of civilization, and if all civilized men unite in harmonious consent to coin it from anything whatsoever, doubtless they could carry out the determination and continue to live It is a question of policy, wise or unwise as such. Probably its wisdom or unwisdom as a policy must depend upon an intelligent understanding of natural laws which men cannot change any more than they can overturn the order of the seasons, but after all it remains for them primarily a question of policy.

In that period of our history the Democratic party became infected with the profound unrest, the passionate yearning for "some new thing" which should be powerful to remove the painful inequalities of condition, the grinding hardships which had been developed in the evolution of civilization and were acutely felt among a people who were earnestly striving to put in practice the yet young theory of self-government. It was the same unrest and longing for something new which four years earlier had burst out in the sudden coalescence of diverse elements into a new party mustering more than a million voters without apparent effort.

During the second Cleveland administration the younger leaders of Democratic sentiment, profoundly disappointed with the results of the only two administrations the party had even nominally secured in more than thirty years, had been diligently studying the situation. They saw that while in 1892 the party with which they were identified had barely held its own in numbers, making no part of the natural gain it should have made in the general growth of population, the opposing party had not only failed of all such natural gain, but had actually suffered a positive loss of more than a quarter of a million votes. They saw that these actual and constructive losses by the dominant parties were coincident, in time, with the sudden growth to a strength of more than a million voters of a new party whose proclaimed principles were largely modifications, expansions in a more radically Democratic direction, of some of their own party theories. They argued that because the growth of this new party had apparently drawn more from their old opponents than from themselves, it would, if its momentum could be sustained, continue to draw from the Republican- party out of its discontented element. The so-called "Liberal Republican" movement had led them,—forgetting that most of the Liberal Republicans were one-time Demo-crats,—to imagine the discontented element in the Republican party to be larger and more dis-contented than it was. They saw little or nothing in the new party's principles or aims to prevent a union between the great mass of their own party and the new party, largely on a basis of the latter's principles and aims, and in such a union of elements which they believed to be kindred enough to assure cohesion for a common end, they persuaded them-selves that they could, and did, see "the promise and potency" of overwhelming defeat of the Republican organization. It seemed to them merely a matter of simple addition that the alliance, apparently easy because of natural kinship, be-tween the Populist and the Democratic parties must of necessity evolve an overwhelming majority adverse to Republican policy.

They secured, therefore, a large proportion, indubitably Democratic, in the Democratic national convention of 1896, and there, a single brilliant oration, addressed mainly to the silver coin-age theory, believed to be common to Populist and Democrat alike, blew the flame of enthusiasm to white heat, and seemed to weld the two par-ties at once into one. The orator who sounded the ringing call to arms for the newly compounded party, was made the nominee of the convention, as every thoughtful man who heard the speech or who read it the next morning must have seen at once would be done.

Bryan, the priest and prophet of this attempt to erect a new political faith out of old creeds, a man of brilliant intellectual gifts, of tremendous personal energy and enthusiasm, and of spotless personal character, entered at once, in his own person, on the campaign. He threw aside all the Old traditions of Presidential campaigns, and undertook the enormous labor of a personal canvass of the whole country, traveling many thou-sands of miles and daily and nightly—one might almost say hourly—speaking to immense and nearly always enthusiastic throngs of people, in which women were often conspicuous. There was much in the campaign to remind old men of the "whirlwind" campaign of 1840, save that now the candidate himself was so steadily the central figure.

McKinley, for many years a leading figure in the advocacy of a protective tariff, was named by the Republican party. A man of ability also, though not the orator as was his opponent, but a far-seeing man with a profound knowledge of men, as spotless in personal character as his adversary, and of an unfailing and most winning personal charm. He did not "take the stump" like his opponent, but be was known to be ready to meet all who chose to go to see him in his central Ohio home, and all through the campaign he had practically no days of quiet and rest, "delegations" without number going to see him and publishing the occasion to every man each one met.

Far more than ever before it was a veritable campaign of education." Bryan preached his coinage doctrine from the stump, and his sup-porters filled the country with printed expositions of its claims and argument in its support. The menace found in his doctrine against the established monetary usages of civilization, stirred the believers in an orderly evolution of civilized business and finance, and those who dreaded the results of a doctrinaire revolution in financial practice, to feverish activity. Thousands of men who ordinarily content themselves with merely voting, and who had not by any means always done even that, gave their time to the organization of "sound money leagues," and their money to paying the expense of printing and disseminating argument, information and appeal into every nook and corner of the land. They found themselves forced by the challenge of the "free silver" propaganda to defend what they had not before supposed to stand in need of defense, and they did it without stint or grudging. No one had ever before dreamed of such a pervading deluge of "campaign literature." Once more, but in a new way, the whole people were stirred to the bottom.

The effect was visible in a surprising degree in the popular vote. The aggregate was larger than that of 1892 by upward of 2,000,000, exceeding the hitherto unequalled gain in 1876 for Tilden. The vote for Bryan exceeded that for Cleveland in 1892 by 734,210, proving on its face that either the Democratic party had failed to make the gain naturally to be expected when the whole people were so aroused, or that one or the other of the two parties to the new fusion had not been able to carry into the union its full strength. Which of these was the more probable explanation became apparent in what was the most surprising feature of the vote, the fact that the Republican vote, or, at least, the vote for McKinley, exceeded that for Harrison in 1892 by very nearly two mil-lions, or, to be more nearly exact, 1,920,373. As very few Populists could be at all expected to vote for McKinley, it was fairly clear that it was not the Populist side of the fusion that failed to "deliver the goods" as the managers hoped.

It was nearly as surprising that, notwithstanding the energy directed toward fusing all opposition to the Republican policy, there were as many "side shows," Prohibition, Socialist, Laborite, and others as in 1888, and more than in 1892, polling nearly 150,000 votes more than in the higher of those two years, or 557,533, as against 411,967, not speaking, of course, of the great Populist vote of 1892 as in any sense a "side show" merely, since it then carried with it the electoral vote of some states.

This time the day of minority Presidents was totally swept aside, as McKinley's plurality over Bryan was 519,952, his majority over all opponents, "side shows" included, 262,429, and his electoral majority correspondingly large.

Clearly a very large percentage of the Democratic party, once distinctively the "hard money" party, was not disposed to follow one kind of that "hard money" at the cost of the other kind toward which nearly all the rest of the civilized world had gravitated.

CHAPTER XVII

The More Recent Campaigns

The campaign of 1896 touched what is in 1908 the high water mark in our record of voting. A few more votes were cast in the following one, but so few, so far below what any normal gain by force of increased population would be, as to serve chiefly to emphasize the falling off of interest in voting among the people at large. No campaign since that of 1876 had so roused the Democratic party, while between the two was the vital difference that the earlier of them tended to unite the party more compactly, and the later operated directly to divide and weaken it. No campaign since the Civil war had so fully drawn out the voting strength of the whole people. The silver men believed, with entire sincerity, that they were leading a great crusade in favor of ' "the plain people." Their opponents believed, just as sincerely, that they were defending that which material civilization had achieved from grave injury by misguided men who were bent on taking a backward step. The crusaders were incited by a great enthusiasm for what they thought a new benefit to mankind. The defenders of what had been gained for mankind believed that gain to be in danger, and this situation put every man of both hosts into the fighting ranks. There were no camp-followers nor malingerers. The result proved that there were nearly a mil-lion more voters who condemned the crusade than there were who supported it, and it was natural that quiet should follow the struggle.

Probably the most noteworthy revelation of the election was that the country contained very many more voters than most observers supposed. For a number of quadrennial periods, when there had been no abnormal thing like a war to affect the aggregate vote, it had grown from period to period about half to three-quarters of a million, once or twice falling considerably below that amount, but not going above it, save from some quite exceptional causes, such as the new zeal and new methods of 1888 stimulated by the lesson given in 1884 as to what a tremendous effect may be worked by a very small popular plurality in a single state.

Now it was revealed that under the strong excitement of a question of immense importance to everybody, nearly or quite a million more voters went to the polls than the most observant man would have supposed to be in the country. It was a comforting fact to know that they were there, though it was irritating to reflect that it demanded something in the nature of a political earthquake to shake them out into sight where they could be counted.

The new administration encountered the war with Spain, not a war to test national strength at all, but one which gave rise to the attempt to make a political issue out of the acquisition of territory, an issue which those who proclaimed it called imperialism. It argued a curious want of knowledge of our own history to make any question about it at all, and especially to treat it as if it were in any wise a new question. It was only a new manifestation, scarcely new even as to form, of the old question of nationalization, of whether the United States is one powerful nation or merely a loose; limited league of a number of small-potato nations, no one of them able to command the respect of the weakest of the older nations.

It seems strange now that anybody could fail to see that the situation made by this war did not raise for us even one question involving an unsettled principle. Jefferson settled the whole question for us a century ago, when he promptly closed with Napoleon's offer of the real estate then known as Louisiana. There is no question of principle possible in the acquisition by the nation of territory which was not involved in that transaction. The only questions that can arise, assuming the acquisition to be admissible under the recognized code of international morals, are questions of policy. All others were settled a century ago so far as precedent can settle anything.

But men are always ready, when there are no real mountains in sight, to do their utmost to make one out of any mole-hill they can see or can imagine, and so there was effort to make a question out of this old difference of constitutional construction, though the attempt always degenerated when debated into a question of pol-icy, when the new Presidential campaign came on two years after the little war closed.

McKinley was named for a second term, and the Democratic convention again put forward Bryan to oppose him. The silver proposition had been so decisively negatived in '96 that there was a quite general feeling that it was dead, yet it was sedulously pushed into the campaign as far as it could be, though there was loud asseveration that imperialism was the primary question at stake. The campaign is too recent to particularize here about how it was conducted, beyond recalling that it had no little vitality injected into it by the nomination for Vice President with McKinley of a man with very definite and positive convictions of his own, who was quite as ready to do battle for them before the open tribunal of the whole people as Bryan had shown himself to be to champion his theories four years before and now again showed himself to be. There is an interesting inside history of this nomination of Roosevelt for the second place, a bit of history which curiously illustrates how the more or less secret scheming of unfriendly politicians may remind one of the declaration that "curses, like chickens, always come home to roost." But that bit of history lies wholly with-in the annals of one party to the campaign alone, and hardly has place in a review of the campaigns themselves further than as the result of the scheming rose to the surface in the course of the contest.

On its face, the only visible result in this way was that for the first time in our history a candidate for the second place took, spontaneously and without apparent effort, before the people of the country a rank very nearly as conspicuous as that accorded to his principal, a fact that became of very great consequence only a little later. Few among the people attached much consequence to the declamation about imperialism, but there was sufficient uneasiness still over the silver proposition to draw out quite a full vote, though not one displaying the aggregate growth which unquestionably took place between 1896 and 1900. There was growth in the aggregate vote, but it was relatively insignificant, that of 1900 exceeding that of 1896 by only 16,886. The vote for each of the two principals, however, showed a gain of something more than the aggregate gain, that of McKinley over his former vote being 110,162, and that for Bryan 71,148. McKinley's plurality over Bryan was 858,966, or nearly 40,000 greater than in 1896. His majority over all opponents, however, was now more than 200,000 greater than before, the aggregate vote for the smaller factions carrying no electoral votes, having fallen off about 160,000, a number not very widely differing from the Palmer and Buckner, or "gold Democrat," vote of 1896. The little factions still went on in their fruitless fluttering, their number this time in-creased by a split in the Prohibition faction, by Socialist Democrats, and Socialist Laborites, and tailing out in a curious little faction called the 'United Christian, which managed to pile up 518 votes. Obviously very much the larger part of the natural gain from new voters had been offset by the neglect of older voters, most of whom, no doubt, were disgruntled Populists on the one side and gold Democrats on the other, but very many of the class of habitual indifferents who felt that they had once taken the trouble to "come out into the open" and slay the silver dragon, and did not feel called upon to take the added trouble to leave their snug retreats merely to stamp on its remains.

Within a few months, and for the third time in 35 years, the sneaking cowards who deal out murder to unarmed and unsuspecting victims, struck down the head of our national government, all of the three distinguished victims having been men who, each in his own way and by reason of his own qualities, stood high in the affectionate regard as well as in the respect and honor of well-nigh the whole people, political foes as well as friends. For some strange perversity of reason, the assassins of rulers of the people, from Cresar to today, have betrayed an astonishing proclivity to pitch upon those who deserved best of mankind.

And now was seen the importance of the fact before adverted to, that the candidate for the second place in the then recent campaign had taken so public a part. Suddenly called upon to take up the burdens of his slaughtered chief, Roosevelt did not come to the ordeal in any wise as an unknown quantity, or a man whose theories of office-bearing had not been made plain. It was soon made reasonably clear that he was keeping his implied, and expressed, pledge to carry out the policy for which his late chief had won the endorsement of the people in the great majority for him of 1900, yet how closely he kept that pledge in conscious view was not fully appreciated until he had, after three years of that fidelity, entered on the discharge of those duties guided by his own convictions only. There is but small doubt that his substantial fidelity in this regard went far to assure the readiness with which his party, when his ostensibly 'vicarious duty was discharged, gave him its approval in a nomination for a term of duty in his own un-mixed right.

The Democratic party, apparently convinced by two defeats, the second more pronounced than the first, under the Populist alliance, now went back to their older type and put forward Alton B. Parker, of New York. It was a strange choice, seeing that so far as he was known at all it was for judicial and not at all political experience, and men instinctively feel that while ability and integrity are alike indispensable in all leading positions, yet some special training and experience in the kind of service to be rendered is equally necessary. A man may be a very able and honorable lawyer, but it does not necessarily follow that he must therefore be a capable preacher, or even laborer.

Again the result of the vote challenges attention and offers to the curious in accounting for seen results from mainly unseen causes a fruitful field for speculation. The aggregate vote no longer showed the gain which had all along been the rule save in exceptional and easily explain-able cases. This time it had suffered a loss of 459,728, though all the states are in the roll and there must have been a large gain of new voters since 1900. Nearly half a million voters, plus all the natural gain, whatever that may have been, refrained from voting at all. The Roosevelt vote, on the other hand, exceeds that for McKinley in 1900 by 404,125, which is not widely different from what seemed the average quadrennial gain of the party twenty years earlier, but is probably 25 to 30 per cent less than it should have been. The vote for Parker fell short of that for Bryan in 1900 by 1,278,113, largely to be accounted for by a wholesale secession of the Populists from the fusion arranged in 1896 and still fairly well observed in 1900. Turning to the vote of the small factions, the impracticables, one may discover where some of these deserters went, but by no means all of them. The Prohibitionists still showed their about a quarter of a million votes, and the Socialist-Labor faction polled 42,000, or 2,000 more than in 1900. But, besides these, a straight Populist ticket polled. 109,811 woful falling off from their more than a million votes in 1892— and the Socialist ticket headed by Debs, which, with the same head in 1900, polled 87,910, now polled 396,619. These 109,811 Watsonites and the surplus of 308,709 Debsites over 1900 probably account for some 400,000 of the loss in the Democratic vote, but many more must be counted among the non-voters.

Since 1896 no appreciable gain has been shown in the aggregate popular vote, though in the four years before that date it swelled more than two and a half millions. In the twelve years between 1896 and 1908 there must have been a legitimate, natural growth of very nearly, if not quite, three million, and perhaps even more. If this year of 1908 calls them out, how will they be divided among the several parties?

CHAPTER XVIII

As Intended And As Conducted

From the most cursory comparison of the course of development of Presidential elections disclosed in even the foregoing outline review of them, with the constitutional provisions for governing them, may be readily seen how much fur-. tiler we have departed from those provisions than the average voter of today suspects, and may furnish such voter—not to speak of the legislator—with much matter for serious and most interesting reflection.

No one can read those provisions, especially in the light of the authoritative exposition of them by Alexander Hamilton in the 68th to the 72nd numbers of the a `Federalist," and in that of the journal of the proceedings of the convention of 1787, without recognizing conclusively certain purposes in the convention relating to the essence of the selection of the President and the manner it laid down for attaining those purposes. First among these, it is plain that the convention in-tended, —and the people of the several states, acting through conventions created for the special purpose of adopting or rejecting the organic law proposed, did, by adopting it, acquiesce in that intention—that the people should voluntarily give up the right and power to choose their chief magistrate to a select body of men, chosen by all to make that selection, and for no other purpose.

The controlling reason appears to have been to avoid the tumults and disorders, the "heats and ferments," as Hamilton called them, which they thought history to teach were inseparable from selections made by the people at large. How far, if at all, they overestimated such danger is not a matter for present consideration, though such election campaigns as those of 1840, of 1860, of 1876 and of 1896 may well lead us to suspect that they were fairly justified in their fears. The immediate point is that in what they did they were guided largely by such apprehensions.

The members of the convention differed on this more than on any other point they had to settle. Of the three so-called "plans" for a constitution first submitted to them, one made no provision of any form of selection, and the other two agreed in confiding the election of the President to Congress. But there were many opinions. Some wished a popular election in each state and "the unit rule" in casting the state's vote. Some proposed a body of electors chosen by the people in defined districts. Some preferred the proposed selection by Congress. Some advocated an election of the

President by a vote of the Governors of the several states. Gouverneur Morris, later a pronounced Federalist, strongly urged a popular vote of the whole people irrespective of state lines or any other divisions. Hamilton advocated an election by the people of the states of a body of electors, who, in their turn, should select another body of electors, who should select the President.

In the "Virginia plan," first adopted in committee of the whole, the power was given to Congress, and that stood until near the end of the convention, save that at one time a body of electors chosen by the State Legislatures was substituted, but after a few days was again replaced by the Congress plan. Only a few days before adjourning the convention gave the election of President and of Vice-President—the latter now first heard of—to a body of electors chosen "in such manner as the Legislatures of the states may direct," and that was the provision adopted.

The only restriction of the power of the Legislatures was that they must not appoint as elector "any Senator, or Representative, or person holding an office of trust or profit under the United States." To Congress was given nothing whatsoever to do with the election of either executive officer, save that it should fix the day when the electors should cast their votes—each state body in its own state—the day when they should themselves be elected (both of which Congress afterwards did), and further, that Congress might determine "by general law" how the certificate of its vote, which each state body of electors must send to the President of the Senate, shall be authenticated. The act of 1792 directed that this authentication should be "by the executive authority" of the state, but gave no hint of how disputes about such authority should be settled.

Further than this, Congress could do nothing, save to sit as witnesses when "the President of the Senate shall, in the presence of the Senate and House of Representatives, open all the certificates, and the votes shall then be counted." There is not a hint that anybody, save only the President of the Senate, shall determine what votes shall be counted. It is made his duty to "open all the certificates" and, obviously, only after he has verified them as lawful votes, can they be counted. To no person whatsoever is there given power to object in any way to the counting of any vote which he, upon opening, directs to be counted.

As early as 1798 an amendment to the constitution was offered in Congress proposing to give that body the power to decide contests about electoral votes, but it was not adopted. Yet that power was assumed and exercised by Congress in the Missouri case in 1821, ever since which time it has assumed to exercise it on more than one occasion, notably in 1876. In 1821, Mr. Clay. then in the House, declared that "the two Houses were called upon to enumerate the votes and, of course, to decide what are votes." They were not, and are not, called upon to do anything of the kind, but only to witness the reception and enumeration of the votes by the President of the Senate, on whom the constitution devolves the duty and the responsibility, clearly meaning to concentrate power and responsibility in one punishable officer, and not scatter both over a large body where the one may be abused and the other evaded without possibility of punishing anybody for the wrong. He asked, with a great show of innocent indignation, if the "House would allow that officer, singly and alone, to decide the question of the legality of the votes," when that was precisely what that officer, the President of the Senate, had done, without question from anybody, for a quarter of a century after the constitution was adopted.

The convention of 1787 made the electors independent officers, each one of whom was clothed with full legal power to vote for any eligible man whomsoever, and theoretically they are so yet. But Congress, having first assumed the power to appoint tellers—whose only legitimate function is arithmetical—then read into that function the power of canvassers (which the Congress itself exercised), and then each party in Congress resolved itself into a party caucus which for twenty or more years "nominated" all Presidential candidates, and by force of party discipline robbed the electors of all discretionary power, the exercise .of which was the very essence of their creation by the convention and acceptance by the states, and forced them to vote only for the caucus nominees.

The confusion, as to party lines, in the elections of 1824 and 1828 broke up the Congressional caucus system, which since 1800 had ruled with a rod of iron, and through "understandings" with the sitting Presidents had restricted Presidential choice to the small "rings" they favored, and absolutely determined in advance every President elected during that period. By 1832 the genius of. Jackson and Van Buren had evolved the "national convention" system instead of the Congressional caucus, and that, with the enormous elaboration of party discipline and party machinery worked out since 1832, remains today. And through it all the elector has been kept, and is yet, the mere puppet, worked by the strings pulled by party managers, which the caucus made him in 1800 and 1804. Bad as was the Congressional caucus system, tainted as it became with chicanery and personal and factional intriguing, it is still an open question whether it was or was not less objectionable, from some points of view at least, than the system that now prevails. It was at least true that while it usurped the power to determine who should be President, all the world knew who and what they were who exercised the power. They held place in the caucus by virtue of first holding responsible official places, and if they abused the power they usurped beyond popular tolerance, the people, knowing whom to strike, could at any election depose them and put others in their places. They knew who were the President-makers and could unseat them, while now, save through vague rumor and repute, they do not know who it may be that governs them by dictating who shall be their official rulers.

The constitution commanded that each state should select electors, equal in number with its Senators and Representatives in Congress, "in such manner as the Legislature thereof may direct." The Legislature might order their election in any way even caprice might hit upon. It might he by popular vote, with a bare majority or a requirement of two-thirds or three-fourths. It might require electors to be chosen by another board of electors, or by any kind of state council. It might direct their appointment by the Governor, with or without legislative assent. It might even direct that they should be chosen by lot, by the turn of a wheel or a throw of dice. Obviously, it might retain the election in itself, and in the earlier years of the Federal government that is precisely what the Legislatures did. It made no difference at first. Everybody was re-solved to vote for Washington in any event. It would have made but little difference with the choice of his successor, John Adams, but for the disturbing influence of Jefferson, with his Jacobinic notions absorbed in France while his com-patriots at home had been, in daily discussions and in the convention of 1787, wrestling with the problem of how to frame a government at once free and stable.

In some of the states changes began early, but in most of them the Legislatures continued to choose electors until after the "era of good feeling." Indeed, as late as 1824 six states, or one-quarter of the whole Union, still did so, and South Carolina hung on to the old practice down to 1868. Until 1824 there was no popular vote for President, and it was not until several years later that it grew to fairly reflect the sentiment of the country.

From 1824 to 1904, inclusive, there were twenty-one Presidential campaigns in which the popular vote can be more or less known, though only approximately in the earlier. In eight of these twenty-one cases the candidate successful in securing a majority of the electoral vote was in a very considerable, sometimes a very large, minority of the whole vote, and in some cases the result was extremely curious in a country where it is supposed "a majority rules." Remark has been made of the campaign of 1876, when a strong interest drew out a full vote, larger than that of four years before by very nearly two millions, yet the successful candidate was defeated before the people by 250,935 votes as between him and his leading competitor, and in the whole vote by 344,833, while that leading competitor had an actual majority in the whole vote of 157,037, yet failed by one vote of a majority of the electoral vote. Four years later a small plurality of but a very few thousand votes for Garfield over Hancock gave him, Garfield, a majority of the electors, though the majority against him in the whole vote was 312,025.

In 1860, with the whole vote divided among four competitors, Mr. Lincoln, with a plurality over either of the other three, secured an electoral majority, though in a minority of 944,149 in the whole vote. Still more curiously, in that same year, Douglas, with nearly two and a half times as many votes as Bell, yet secured only 12 electoral votes against Bell's 39.

Again, in 1884, Cleveland's plurality of 23,005 over Blaine gave him an electoral majority, though the majority against him in the whole vote was 300,734. Still more curiously, in the next election, in 1888, Cleveland, though given a plurality over his leading competitor, Harrison, of 96,658, was beaten in the whole vote by 315,309, and the man whom he led nearly 100,000 in the popular vote defeated him in the electoral vote. And yet more strangely than this, apparently because of the sudden rise of a new party in the next campaign, in 1892, Cleveland, given a plurality over his leading competitor, again Harrison, of 366,211, secured with that plurality an electoral majority, though in the whole vote there was a majority against him of 954,891 votes.

Thus it appears that during the twenty or more years while the State Legislatures chose the electors and the Congressional caucus dictated the candidates to whom the electors must confine their votes, the people at large had no voice in choosing their President save indirectly and remotely in their choice of state and national legislators, and the electors were reduced from the free agents the constitution intended they should be to mere nullities, doing the bidding of the caucus. In 1828 the caucus, ostensibly in the interest of "the masses," had been killed, and the nominations were made by the State Legislatures, about one-fourth of them still choosing the electors,

Then the national party convention system was evolved, through which, in theory, the people a. large, acting through these conventions, were supposed to assume the nomination of candidates, and in the great majority of the states—since 1868 in all—the electors were and are chosen by popular vote under the direction of the Legislatures of the states. But the change brought no more freedom to the electors. Before the change they did the bidding of the caucus. Since the change they have done that of the conventions, and who finally determines that bidding nobody knows with certainty.

And yet, nullities and puppets though they are, in more than one-third of the elections held in the 84 years following 1820, the necessity for casting the decisive vote for President according to the number and localities, by states, of the electors, in order to meet the form of the constitutional requirement, has in effect nullified and defeated "the will of the people," to promote which the convention system was supposed to be created. Eight times within that period, if the vote of the people had been counted directly in-stead of being strained and sifted through the meshes of the electoral college, the country would have had a different President from him it had on each of these occasions, and more than once in those eight times would have had no President save through the action of the House of Representatives, unless a plurality had been per-mitted to prevail.

Most of all, it appears, from even a cursory analysis of this review, that save for the un-certain check on popular excitement arising from the knowledge in the people of the necessity, be-hind the direct act of voting, of complying with the forms and the numerical count of the electoral system, we have been, every four years in all those 84 years, exposed to all the dangers of those "heats and ferments," that liability to turbulence and disorder, so much dreaded by the framers of the constitution, the strong desire to escape which was their controlling motive and inspiration in devising the indirect method of the electoral system. It is hard to see, looking back-ward to 1824, how we could have been more ex-posed to dangerous "heats and ferments" than we have been, even if Gouverneur Morris had prevailed in persuading the convention to pro-vide for the election of the President by a direct vote en masse of the whole people.

It may well be, as the framers of the constitution thought, and many still think, that it is not wise always to give free course to the instant "will of the people," because, like individuals, they are prone to do, in moments of passion, what their "sober second thought' regrets. And if it be held wise to guard against this liability, there is comfort in the reflection that though Congress and political parties have both tried to deprive the electoral device of the force intended for it, and have robbed the electors of their individual free agency, there has still survived in the observance of its mere forms a barrier able to check the flow of heady passion and give men time for reflection and more deliberate action. Yet beyond these reflections there are two conclusions in which we seem to be fairly justified by the experience of a hundred and twenty years, both of them encouraging to those who hope for the survival and substantial success of free political institutions among men.

The first, and perhaps the more solidly encouraging of the two, is that all the changes in the forms and agencies of political action through which we have passed since the constitution was adopted, have been almost, one may say entirely, in the nature of evolution and not at all of revolution. There are Political communities assuming, and probably honestly thinking themselves, to be free, in which the first impulse of an earnest party when it finds itself defeated at the polls, is to hunt for its guns and, with loud protestations of having been defrauded, to set about overruling the ballot with bullets. The people of the United States have never shown that disposition. Once, indeed, a large part of the nation attempted revolution by war, but openly, frankly, and with orderly deliberation, and when their appeal to the sword failed, they accepted the adverse decree as brave and honorable men.

The framers of the constitution provided for the selection of the nation's executive bead by a body of men to be chosen by the states in any manner their legislatures might direct. Had they contemplated that the whole people should indicate at till for whom those men should vote, they would assuredly have provided the means by which such indication should be made by the people. They were men of too much wisdom to have omitted site''' precaution.

Their error lay in not foreseeing that the people would not be content to be bound in electing Presidents by the action of their legislatures, bodies of men not chosen with that end at all in view. As was inevitable, when the one man revered above all others had served out his term, the determination of political action became at once a matter of parties, and it was of course an imperative necessity that some means should he found by which each party could assure unity of action in its own ranks.

The congressional caucus of the representative men of each party, was in large measure, one might say wholly, a spontaneous response to that demand. Spontaneous action among the people at large was obviously uncertain and difficult. and grew more so as the nation grew in population, and even if it could he had. a party's strength was likely to be wasted on half a dozen or More dates. No one man or one party invented the congressional caucus. It was a spontaneous growth, a genuine fruit of evolution, and for twenty or more years the people acquiesced in its action.

As has been seen, there were reasons why it did not fairly and fully meet the demand out of which it grew.

Then, for one or two terms, there was doubt and uncertainty. The state legislatures assumed the unifying function, but each was narrowly local, and unity of action among them was well-nigh as impossible as among the individuals of the people. Obviously the authority to nominate must be as wide as the party.

The party convention was another response to the

demand for unity of action, and was as little the invention of any one man or one party. Various efforts were made toward it between 1810 and 1.832, but they all fell more or less short of their aim until the organizing genius of Van Buren and the immense, popularity of Jackson in one party and Clay in the other welded it into a well-defined instrument of Political action.

Again here was—and still is—a fruit of orderly evolution, not at all the dictum of any autocrat imposed on the people, nor the fiat of any self-seeking conspirators. Beyond doubt it may, for a time, be abused by corrupt and designing men, but in essence it is democratic, and the whole people may at any time make it what they will. Surely there is encouragement in that ultimate truth.

The second encouraging conclusion is that with all the imperfections of the electoral system, though the constitutional aim of independent electors has been evaded, though congress has "meddled" unpardonably, first through its nominating caucus and later in other ways that have been indicated, notwithstanding all this and all that has been alleged against the party "machine," never yet has the election system placed a really had man in the president's seat. Scrutinize the long role of chief magistrates as we may, though some have been stronger and better officials and men than others, and some were nominated, for supposed "availability" over stronger men than themselves, not one has been of the type which, among the rulers of nations, could fairly be set down as a vicious man, not one who can even be classed as a weak man, while some, who it was feared might prove weak, have greatly risen to great occasions when confronted by them. Is there any other list of consecutive rulers of a great nation? fairly equivalent in numbers and in time, of whom more of good may be said with equal truth?

www.ingramcontent.com/pod-product-compliance
Lightning Source LLC
Chambersburg PA
CBHW060456280326
41933CB00014B/2772